The Agony of a People

Armenians in the Modern and Early Modern World

Recent decades have seen the expansion of Armenian Studies from insular history to a broader, more interactive field within an inter-regional and global context. This series, Armenians in the Modern and Early Modern World, responds to this growth by promoting innovative and interdisciplinary approaches to Armenian history, politics, and culture in the period between 1500-2000. Focusing on the geographies of the Mediterranean, Middle East, and Contemporary Russia [Eastern Armenia], it directs specific attention to imperial and post-imperial frameworks: from the Ottoman Empire to Modern Turkey/Arab Middle East; the Safavid/Qajar Empires to Iran; and the Russian Empire to Soviet Union/Post-Soviet territories.

Series Editor
Bedross Der Matossian, *University of Nebraska, Lincoln, USA*

Advisory Board
Levon Abrahamian, *Yerevan State University, Armenia*
Sylvie Alajaji, *Franklin & Marshal College, USA*
Sebouh Aslanian, *University of California, Los Angeles, USA*
Stephan Astourian, *University of California, Berkley, USA*
Houri Berberian, *University of California, Irvine, USA*
Talar Chahinian, *University of California, Irvine, USA*
Rachel Goshgarian, *Lafayette College, USA*
Ronald Grigor Suny, *University of Michigan, USA*
Sossie Kasbarian, *University of Stirling, UK*
Christina Maranci, *Tufts University, USA*
Tsolin Nalbantian, *Leiden University, the Netherlands*
Anna Ohanyan, *Stonehill College, USA*
Hratch Tchilingirian, *University of Oxford, UK*

Published and Forthcoming Titles
The Armenian Genocide and Turkey: Public Memory and Institutionalized Denial, Hakan Seckinelgin
The Armenian Women's Movement in the Late Ottoman Empire: Modernity, Nationalism and Gender, Hasmik Khalapyan

The Agony of a People

*Haig Toroyan's Eyewitness Account of
the Armenian Genocide*

Zabel Yesayan
Translated from the Western Armenian by Arakel Minassian
Translation edited by Maral Aktokmakyan and Tamar Boyadjian

I.B. TAURIS

I.B. TAURIS
Bloomsbury Publishing Plc
50 Bedford Square, London, WC1B 3DP, UK
1385 Broadway, New York, NY 10018, USA
29 Earlsfort Terrace, Dublin 2, Ireland

BLOOMSBURY, I.B. TAURIS and the I.B. Tauris logo are trademarks of Bloomsbury Publishing Plc

First published in Great Britain 2025

Copyright © Marc Nichanian, 2025
Introduction © Elyse Semerdjian, 2025
Translation by © Arakel Minassian, 2025

Marc Nichanian, Elyse Semerdjian, and Arakel Minassian have asserted their right under the Copyright, Designs and Patents Act, 1988, to be identified as Authors of the Introduction work.

For legal purposes, the Acknowledgments on p. xi constitute an extension of this copyright page.

Series design by Adriana Brioso
Cover image: American Committee for Armenian and Syrian Relief [165-VV-559C-33], courtesy of the National Archives and Records Administration

All rights reserved. No part of this publication may be reproduced or transmitted in any form or by any means, electronic or mechanical, including photocopying, recording, or any information storage or retrieval system, without prior permission in writing from the publishers.

Bloomsbury Publishing Plc does not have any control over, or responsibility for, any third-party websites referred to or in this book. All internet addresses given in this book were correct at the time of going to press. The author and publisher regret any inconvenience caused if addresses have changed or sites have ceased to exist, but can accept no responsibility for any such changes.

A catalogue record for this book is available from the British Library.

A catalog record for this book is available from the Library of Congress.

ISBN: HB: 978-0-7556-5430-7
PB: 978-0-7556-5431-4
ePDF: 978-0-7556-5433-8
eBook: 978-0-7556-5432-1

Typeset by Deanta Global Publishing Services, Chennai, India

Series: Armenians in the Modern and Early Modern World

To find out more about our authors and books visit www.bloomsbury.com and sign up for our newsletters.

To the memory of my great-uncle, Haig Toroyan

Contents

List of Figures	x
Editor's Acknowledgments	xi
Translator's Preface	xv
Translating *Hokevark* or the Untranslatable Life-form *Maral Aktokmakyan*	xviii
Between the Lines: Haig Toroyan's Testimony and the Armenian Genocide *Elyse Semerdjian*	xxiii
Note on Transliteration	xxx

	Introduction by Zabel Yesayan from Original Publication in Korz, February and March 1917, Baku	1
1	Dikranagerd, November 1914. Economic Boycott. The Burning of the Bazaar. Military Requisitions and Mobilization.	3
2	Jarābulus, December 1914 to November 12, 1915. The Condition of the Armenians Until February 1915. The First Signs of Enmity. The Attempt to Massacre 2,000 Armenian Workers. The Incident of the Loggers.	9
3	The Deportations in Cilicia: Zeytun, Dört-yol (Chork Marzvan). Hajin. Aintab.	13
4	The Story of a Wealthy Village. The Sight of the Arriving Refugees. The Collapsed Woman. Nighttime Assaults. A Complaint to the Turkish Authorities.	21
5	An Armenian Mother. Children Are Sold Off. The Role of a Greek Woman.	29
6	The Distribution of Bread. The First Corpses on the Euphrates. Seventy Children Drowned.	35
7	Episodes from the Deportations of Armenians from Armenia. Dikranagerd. Mardin. In Resulayn. In Tell Abyad. In Edessa. Arap Pınar.	41

8   *The Plain of Suruç/Suruj Plain* (Armenian Cemetery). Jarābulus's Bazaar. The Image of the Nizib *Khan*. 51

9   The Transportation of the Population by Train. Water . . . Water . . . A Woman from Yerznga, and the Deportation of Yerznga. The Story of Chemeshgadzak. 57

10 The Deported Population on Foot Toward Aleppo. A Bride's Escape. The Passage of Seventy Armenians from Erzrum (the Deportation of Erzrum). 65

11 Groups of Armenians Passing through Birecik. Murad, Murad, You Have Fulfilled Our Wishes. 71

12 Aleppo. Turkish and Armenian Committees for Settling the Deportees. The Behavior of Aleppo's Armenian Population. The Condition of Aleppo's Armenian Population. A General Picture. The Passage of the Armenian Intellectuals. Zohrab and Vartkes. 75

13 The Edessa (Urfa) Resistance. The First Steps of Deportation. The Armenians Are in Revolt. Negotiations. A Turkish Army Besieges the Armenian Quarter. Fifteen Days of Fighting. Edessa Ruined. The Former Situation. 83

14 A Wedding Among the Kurds. A Temporary Order Concerning the Property of the Exiled Armenians. The Birecik Armenians Convert to Islam, yet Are Still Deported. The Words of a Turkish Soldier from Marash. 89

15 The Turks' Suspicious Attitude Toward Me and the Other Local Armenians. Jarābulus's the German Hospital at Jarābulus. Captain Otto Oehlmann, a German Officer. My Departure. 93

16 Meskene. The Teacher. Toward Raqqa. 97

17 Raqqa. The Armenian Cemetery. The Sight of the People Gone Mad in the Field. The State of the Exiles on the Left Bank in Raqqa. The Burial of a Girl. 103

18 Toward Deir ez-Zor. Marash's Armenian Villagers. The Image of the Population on the Banks of the Euphrates. A Second Meeting with a Group of Armenian Exiles. 109

19	Deir ez-Zor. Meeting with the Colonel. The Market. A Girl from Mezere. Before the Pharmacy.	113
20	Toward Anē. Anē. An Old Man Loses Consciousness. The Market.	117
21	Toward Hadise. Hadise. The Price of Freeing an Armenian Girl.	119
22	Hīt. The Students of Aintab's Seminary. The Market. An Armenian Girl Is Requested from Baghdad.	121
23	Ramadi. 300 Armenians from Zeytun in a Cave. The Conduct of an Arab Baker. Fallujah. The Story of a Wealthy Armenian Family.	123
24	Baghdad. Forty-nine Armenians Are Deported. The Gallows. The Armenians' Situation. The German Consul's Resistance. The Words of Halil Pasha.	127
25	Toward Persia. The Arabs Steal Two Trunks of Weapons. We Cross the Border. The German Officer Takes to Illness. He Goes Mad. Toward Kermanshah. The German Officer Commits Suicide. The Russians Capture Kermanshah, and I Go to the Caucasus.	129
Afterword: Testimony and Authorship: Zabel Yesayan's *The Agony of a People:* Written by Marc Nichanian, translated by Tamar M. Boyadjian		137
Index		159

Figures

To the memory of my great-uncle, Haig Toroyan   v
Haig Toroyan, seated on the left, with his brother Aram and sisters Armenouhi (left) and Haiganoush (right)   xi

Editor's Acknowledgments

First, I need to thank Tamar Boyadjian and Maral Aktokmakyan, who acted as editors and advisers for this text, coming into the process at just the right time to ensure that it would be as strong as possible. I am forever grateful for their work and support.

In 1912, my great-grandmother Armenouhi Toroyan Manoogian left her home in Aleppo, Syria, and sailed to America with her four-year-old daughter, Azadouhi. They were following Armenouhi's husband, Bedros, who had left two years earlier after being drafted into the Ottoman Army. For Armenians at that time, this meant certain death.

Haig Toroyan, seated on the left, with his brother Aram and sisters Armenouhi (left) and Haiganoush (right)

Armenouhi left behind her parents and six siblings. While her youngest brother, Henry, eventually emigrated to America, she never saw the others again.

This young family eventually made their way to Watertown, Massachusetts, and had three more children. The youngest was my grandmother, Isabel.

Unfortunately, neither of my great-grandparents lived a long life nor did their youngest child. My grandmother Isabel passed away when I was just three years old. Luckily, the child who came with her parents from Aleppo in 1912, Azadouhi, lived until I was in my late teens. We called her "Auntie Zee." It was in her living room in East Watertown that I learned the stories of our family.

A feature of many stories was her uncle Haig. Auntie Zee told stories of him taking bread to Armenians in the desert in 1915. Of hiding Armenians in the train station that his brother ran in Aleppo, to bring them to safety. She often told us that Uncle Haig wrote a book. These stories made their way in letters from Aleppo to Watertown in the 1920s and 1930s; no one in my family had ever seen the book.

Nearly twenty years after Azadouhi passed away, I was finally able to track down Uncle Haig's book. While our family had never seen it, it soon became clear that much of the Armenian world had.

Thanks to the work of noted philosopher and professor of Armenian literature Marc Nichanian, I was able to read quotes from Haig's work in English via a digitized version of his *Writers of Disaster: Armenian Literature in the Twentieth Century* (2002).

I learned that from November 1915 to January 1916, Haig Toroyan had traveled down the Euphrates disguised as the Christian Arab translator for a German military official. He saw the death marches and camps of the Armenians—his own people. While hiding his identity, he would encounter his own relatives among the deported, knowing he could not help them. In early 1916, he told his firsthand testimony to prominent Armenian intellectual Zabel Yesayan. In February and March of 1917, Yesayan published his account in Kordz, a monthly journal in Baku. It was the first published eyewitness account in the aftermath of the Genocide of 1915.

Again, thanks to Marc Nichanian, sometime in 2008, I finally had a photocopied version of *Agony of a People* in my hands in its original Western Armenian.

I knew I wanted to have Haig's words translated into English—at the very least so my non-Armenian-reading family could read them. However, once I realized how important this first-ever testimony was, I hoped I could bring it to an even wider audience.

There were several key people who helped me reach this point. First and foremost, Marc Nichanian, who has carried Haig's testimony forward, including it in his books and lectures, translating it to French and publishing L'Agonie d'un peuple in 2013. Marc answered that first email from me—a stranger claiming to be Haig Toroyan's great-niece—with immediate warmth and connection. He has encouraged me and helped shepherd this English translation at every step.

This work would also not be possible without Judy Saryan, a Zabel Yesayan scholar I hoped would know about Haig's work and she did! Judy brought me into her home for dinners with local Armenian and Genocide scholars and eventually helped me find our translator. She has partnered on this project and helped me navigate the world of Western Armenian translation, and she has always been available to answer my questions, offer any support I needed or to simply cheer me on.

I am also eternally grateful for our translator and the amazing work he has done. I met Arakel Minassian at Judy's dinner table in the summer of 2019. We had no idea a worldwide pandemic was about to occur, but Arakel stayed the course through all the disruptions and delivered a fantastic translation.

In the final stages of this work, I have been lucky enough to meet and work with Bedross Der Matossian, professor and past president of the Society of Armenian Studies, as well as the series editor of Armenians in the Modern and Early Modern World published by I.B. Tauris and Bloomsbury Press. Talar Chahinian, author and scholar, evaluated and edited our final product. Talar and Bedross were incredibly kind and patiently worked with me as I navigated the world of translation and academic publishing.

I also owe thanks to Elyse Semerdjian, the Robert Aram and Marianne Kaloosdian and Stephen and Marian Mugar Chair of Armenian Genocide Studies at the Strassler Center for Holocaust and Genocide Studies at Clark University, for offering her time to write an introduction. Elyse's piece, setting the historical context during which Zabel and Haig were living, is very important.

Getting the place names in Ottoman Turkey translated correctly was also essential, and I have Ani Boghikian Kasparian, from the University of Michigan-Dearborn Armenian Research Center and the Houshamadyan Project, to thank for her expertise.

In addition to my acknowledgment, I must again thank Tamar Boyadjian and Maral Aktokmakyan. Tamar Boyadjian translated Marc Nichanian's Western Armenian introduction to Agony of a People, as it felt right to keep his words alongside this new translation. And Maral Aktokmakyan brought her perspective as a scholar of Western Armenian literature, as well as pre- and post-Genocide Ottoman Armenians to a new introduction. Not only did they contribute to this piece through their work, but they also offered encouragement and support as I guided this book to publication.

This publication was also made possible with generous funding from the National Association for Armenian Studies and Research (NAASR). I cannot thank them enough for seeing the value in this project.

Lastly, this English translation would not have come to fruition without the encouragement and help from my family. My grandmother has been gone for more than forty-five years, but her three daughters—my mom and her sisters—consistently supported me and this project. And of course, my Auntie Zee: without her stories I would never have known about my uncle Haig or his powerful testimony.

Jennifer Langley
Boston, Massachusetts
June 2024

Translator's Preface

When I was first approached about translating Zabel Yesayan's *The Agony of a People*, I jumped at the opportunity to work on such a remarkable figure. I began by translating Yesayan's preface and a brief sample of the first chapter. The preface was clearly written in Yesayan's own pen and from her voice—the language and style were reminiscent of the long and powerful sentences characteristic of her preface to *Among the Ruins*. Yet as I moved into the testimony itself, the language suddenly changed, and I was confronted at this earliest stage with the question of who I was translating—was this Zabel Yesayan or Haig Toroyan? Was it both?

Although the byline of *The Agony of a People* reads Zabel Yesayan, the author herself notes in her preface that this is the eyewitness testimony of a man named Haig Toroyan, and that she has written this account in the first person, from his perspective. So in translating, whose voice was I to inhabit? Who was speaking? But there was a second and related problem. This was not simply Toroyan's testimony of his own experiences. His position as interpreter allowed him to speak with just about everyone (Turks, Kurds, Arabs, Armenians, and Assyrians), and in addition to what he himself had witnessed, Toroyan also gives us the accounts of others in full detail and often written in Yesayan's piece from their first-person perspective. Sometimes these accounts are marked by quotation marks, but at other times, Toroyan's testimony bleeds seamlessly into another's account. What is more, these accounts often switch unexpectedly between past and present, at times even within one individual's testimony. So there were several layers of difficulty here, especially when I considered rendering this into "smooth" and "readable" English. How could such a disjointed account be brought into English without sounding strange or foreign? Was it better to make the accounts uniform, to "smooth out the rough edges," as it were?

I ultimately decided, as you will see in the translation that follows, to maintain the disjointed narrative I saw in Armenian. There were moments when I thought the piece could benefit from making the tense more uniform, but for the most part, I knew something would be missing if I departed too much from how the text was written. I confess to not quite understanding at the time why *The Agony of a People* was written as it was, and I am not convinced even now that this was intentional. Nonetheless, I would suggest that the way this testimony was written tells us something significant about the story and about this moment in history, and I therefore could not erase the broken nature of this testimony in translation.

To elaborate on this issue, we need to return to the circumstances surrounding the writing of *The Agony of a People*. Haig Toroyan says repeatedly in his testimony that he recorded everything in his notebook. Toroyan met Yesayan in Baku in 1916, and in *The Agony of a People*'s very first footnote, Yesayan says that this is Toroyan's own testimony, which he spoke to her and which she wrote down: "The following pages are written in the first person, because they are Mr. Toroyan's oral descriptions and impressions, which I have written down." Yesayan gives the impression that Toroyan sat down with her and spoke this testimony while she wrote. Surely, this would have been the case to a certain degree, but we also know that Yesayan had access to Toroyan's notebooks and actually took them with her to Paris.[1] In any case, although Toroyan could have remembered all he had seen by heart, it is far more likely that he had to remind himself of some of the events by looking at his notes, and since we know Yesayan had access to the notebooks as well, it is likely that she drew on his own writing as she wrote and edited. Some accounts from his notebook may have made it directly into the piece in the voices of those recorded, as we see so often in this book.

I dwell on this point to say that the preparation of this testimony must have required considerable effort, a stitching together of different accounts in addition to the remembrances of someone who had just witnessed unspeakable horrors. The very disjointed nature of this testimony, the jumping between perspectives and time, tells us about the difficulty of writing this experience, of putting this account together into a single storyline. The narrative therefore enacts the very preparation of compiling and writing this testimony, and it was thus imperative for this brokenness to follow its original into English translation. At the end of the day, no matter what ideas and theories of translation I held before I started working, no matter what I could imagine as the demands of an English readership, I could only go as far as the text would allow me to. The text itself conditioned the manner in which I translated, and I found myself returning again and again to the parameters Toroyan and Yesayan had set for me.

---

[1] This is elaborated in detail by Marc Nichanian's preface to the 2022 Armenian edition published by Aras Press in Turkey. The preface is included in this edition as well.

Translator's Preface   xvii

In translating this piece, I worked directly from the original copy of *Zhoghovurti mě hokevark'ě* as it was printed in the two issues of Kordz in 1917, which were available electronically through the National Library of Armenia. I also referred often to Marc Nichanian's 2013 French translation, which was often helpful as a "sounding board" (as it were) for my own translation choices. For historical background, I referred primarily to Raymond Kevorkian's *The Armenian Genocide: A Complete History* and Ronald Suny's *They Can Live in the Desert but Nowhere Else: A History of the Armenian Genocide*, both of which helped me contextualize the eyewitness accounts I was translating.

Translation is rarely an individual endeavor, and in addition to the published aids that contributed to my work, I am grateful for the help and advice I received from friends and colleagues along the way. Michael Pifer, my mentor and friend at the University of Michigan, was always there to answer linguistic questions and provided important guidance as the book neared publication. Other friends I often turned to for linguistic and historical context included Armen Abkarian, Erin Piñon, and Anahit Ghazaryan. I am also grateful for the counsel and support of Jennifer Manoukian in the later stages of publication.

None of this would have been possible without the tireless and devoted work of Jen Langley, who financially supported the project and did the significant organizational labor of making sure this translation made it to completion. I am so grateful that she continued to trust me, especially through the difficulties of the pandemic and all the other setbacks that appeared along the way.

Lastly, I could not have finished this translation without the support of my parents and my partner, Sara Ruiz. Sara was the first reader of most of this translation and was always ready to advise me on how my choices came across in English. She supported me in more ways than I can count, and I am so grateful to have had her with me throughout this process.

Arakel Minassian
Ann Arbor, Michigan
February 26, 2024

Translating *Hokevark* or the Untranslatable Life-form[1]

Maral Aktokmakyan

What would Zabel Yesayan's literature be like, if she were born and claimed by a different nation in a politically peaceful corner of the world, in an environment that was humane, instead of the place where she lived, where, through and through, she witnessed an almost endless streak of violence, atrocities, massacres, and other inhumane ruptures? There's no doubt that she would still end up becoming a well-known writer—as she would still prioritize the human condition in her artistic productions; and she would still portray a fragment of human life with her innate talent to penetrate to the depths of the psyche and inner world of her characters. Her genius lies in capturing the moments of standing on the threshold, in the way she renders visibility of what it means to be "human." Yesayan, in this sense, is the perfect translator of what can be called the "human condition": any state that is stuck in-between life and death, between living and dying, between life as human action and life as labor. She excels, every time, in bringing almost an untranslatable and irreducible experience of "human life" into her writing. Her desire to interpret the human, in all its forms, is evident from her earliest works, during her time in Paris (Կեղծ Հանճարներ, Հոգներն և Շշունջներր) up to her last unfinished works (Բարպա Խաչիկ). It is not a coincidence that in each work, Yesayan plays with the idea of the human either as the main theme or as a secondary one, set in the backdrop of Paris, Istanbul, or Adana.

Let us turn back from the opening question to the reality of her times. From her childhood days onward, Yesayan witnessed not one but several instances where human life for Armenians pushed the boundaries in ways one could not even imagine in a *civilized* world. The Cilician massacres of 1909 became her first real engagement with such an event which exceptionally threatened the meaning of

---

[1] I'd like to thank Dr. Tamar M. Boyadjian for encouraging me to write this preface, which has been part of our discussions, and Jennifer Langley for her support and comments on an earlier version of this chapter.

the human quality of life. She penned the literary testimony entitled *Among the Ruins*, which came out only in 1911. This work was then followed—among many other testimonies—by "The Orphanages of Cilicia"; and in 1917, by three main testimonies: *The Agony of a People*, *Murat's Journey (from Sivas to Batum)*, and *Nor Sepastia*. Nichanian presents meticulous research; he reviews the realities in which Yesayan wrote down Hayg Toroyan's testimony, unfolding each and every detail, almost like a jigsaw puzzle, telling us also the importance of writing Toroyan's testimony under the disguise of his person and voice. In Nichanian's introduction, the reader will be taken on a journey among the philosophical concepts around the writing of this testimony and the paradoxical position of the witness. The reader will be led to understand these circumstances through Yesayan's experience as a woman, intellectual, writer, and reporter-translator.

And here, on this very page, the reader finds a quagmire, by reading yet another preface that opens itself as a "preface of another preface," which pre-speaks for *the* preface written by Yesayan. In the traditional sense, the philosophical idea of a preface is said to be submissive in "nature." Accordingly, a preface is solely entitled to prepare the reader for a reading, or more correctly a pre-reading. While the main text is always regarded as authentic, a preface can only get a secondary status by its essence. It surely derives from the idea that a preface imitates and repeats what is to be said in the "original" text—that which is yet to come. The inferiority imposed upon the idea of prefatory writing also brings forth the question of self-negation and self-ghosting: a preface is supposed to be silent and by its essence, it is only allowed to be absent as a "pre-text." It is hardly ever expected that a preface should take on the sovereign act of extrapolating the text upon itself, and convey and spread the original word or message that lies embedded in the main text. And prefaces such as the one by the genius pen of Yesayan reveal more than the sole function of delivering the foreword of the original book. Yesayan reforms the space of her own prefatory note into an original space, equating its role in the "what-is-to-come," which unfolds other spheres and meanings, even before the primary text. And how did she manage to twist and turn the meaning and role of the preface? Respecting the limits of *this*—very traditional—preface, the present brief analysis will only be restricted to the title of this work: *The Agony of a People*, as it is translated in this book for the English reader. Clearly, Yesayan did not use any Armenian words equivalent to "agony," nor did she use expressions such as "sorrow," "pain," "suffering," or "torment." She also avoided using the word "death" to describe the dire situation of her people. Instead, she preferred to characterize this singular experience narrated with the unique Armenian word *հոգեվարք / hokevark*. Her word choice makes her perspective, as well as her sensibility and art, so invaluable—as using this word opens up many nuances in meaning. The untranslatable state of *hokevark*—that which is neither being in life nor being in death— avoids being attached to a resolution or a finite ending. The "dying breath," one of the few ways to interpret this word, keeps the fate of the whole nation, or the Armenian people, separate from an official state that would recognize and lawfully defend them, remaining on the threshold of life and death. This threshold, implied within the word *hokevark*, surely points to the fatal damage and the effect of the genocidal will upon the Armenian people; at the same time, this word keeps the gate open for the possibility of keeping the breath and life alive, simultaneously, with almost the implication of a miraculous return to life for the Armenian people. True that people are mortal, but they are not finished yet; they still have their last breaths and souls—especially the Armenian exiles, whose story Yesayan records on the brink of their death. With this word, we think of a moment frozen in time, right before the last moment, the last breath—before a vulnerable state of still living. Yesayan seems to have described that moment just as a photographer would capture it, set it, and encapsulate it, in time—as to delay the endpoint so that it does not yet finish. Her pen allows the reader to focus completely on the experiences, witnesses, and testimony of Hayk Toroyan, who is enabled to speak and tell us the story of his witnessing, the story of attesting to that moment in time.

Yesayan showed herself as a writer through her rather short appearance in her preface and through her decision on the title. The rest is Toroyan's history, as she has penned it. Her persona and authorial voice have both been effaced, disappeared, and restricted in the whole narrative. Reading page after page, witnessing works in double grounds as well: along with turning ourselves as witnesses of Toroyan's testimony, reading the whole book also manifests the way Yesayan becomes the "caregiver" of Toroyan's testimony, with such simplicity, directness, and selfless fashion. There is not one line where one can even catch a glimpse of Yesayan's sophisticated literary style. Hundreds of descriptions of those human beings are recounted as plainly as possible for the duty of encapsulating "human life" itself, which was dragged out of its supposed meaning.

Yet this was not the first time that she revealed her dutiful approach. Before this testimony, in 1911, when she published *Among the Ruins*, she spoke in and through the preface: "as a free citizen, as an authentic daughter of my country, with the same rights and duties that everyone has." Her reference was to the Ottoman Empire, and she utilized the prefatory space, again—unsurprisingly— writing in Armenian, addressing the new politics emerging under the hand of the Young Turks, who also played their part in the event of the Cilician massacres, prior to the Genocide. Before the main text of *Among the Ruins*, Yesayan transforms the two-and-a-half-page long space of her own preface into a space where she would be able to confront the new political will that officially ended her own political state of being.

Through that space, she replies to the perpetrators who not only caused the massacre of more than 20,000 Armenians in the Cilician region but also brought an end to Yesayan's own political body and life as a citizen of the empire. Just as the paradox of the witness, Yesayan's final say within the limits of her preface also marked the striking paradox of living and dying, speaking as a citizen for the very last time and speaking about her death as a political animal (*zôon politikon*). The preface also resurrected the state of a mere biological being—one that she, herself, became reduced to. Without the *bios* (or the political life) one would only be recognized as a *zoe* (mere biological life of every living being); according to ancient Greek thought, life was divided and understood through these two categories. It was the last time that she raised her voice as a citizen, against the betrayal of the Young Turks. But the problem was that a voice that was raised and responded to in the preface was the statement about the loss of her political identity, the annihilation of her very being. Somehow, announcing her death, she was addressing her state of being as a political animal for the last time. And how about the rest? True that in what would be considered "the rest" a certain first-person singular narrator speaks; but line by line the testimony, in its entirety, is dedicated to the living life of those Armenians struck by the genocidal will of the perpetrators.

Similarly, Yesayan maintains this same approach also in undertaking the task of writing Toroyan's testimony. True, she chooses to move her pen like a translator as she becomes the "scribe" of the testimonies of Toroyan and other survivors; she manages to do all of this in such a way that she effaces her agency in order to spotlight the very thing that forms the human condition—nothing but the story of human life itself. She contents herself with the constraints of a pre-text and she ghosts herself. But this self-effacing decision in her preface already contradicts itself when her voice, squeezed in the tight space of a "preface," surpasses that secondary, translatory, prefatory status by pointing to the one that will come, to the one that speaks before and beyond. True that Yesayan cancels her visibility as an Armenian, as a woman, a writer, a translator—as Nichanian tells us—only to be able to become a g/host. Who would offer hospitality for this particular state of otherness to speak of and make visible its narrative testimony? If Yesayan's brilliance is still in question, it is this ethical "economy" that she could so adeptly engage herself with, in every political gesture she took as well as in her writing. And she knew the necessity of hospitality. She knew what it meant to grant room for the interpolated experience of having to name what was occurring in these pages, what she called *hokevark*: the dying breath, the death throes, the dying song. These are only some of the phrases that—instead of denying, ignoring, reducing—are capable of conveying the philosophical depth that ruled the state of the Armenian people. And it is through this one word alone that she brings together all that is impossible to translate, all that would be impossible to pen as an experience: as a witness. And so, as always, Zabel Yesayan forged a niche to embed her own voice and save the lives of her own people by helping them survive, literally: through her word and her pen.

Between the Lines: Haig Toroyan's Testimony and the Armenian Genocide

Elyse Semerdjian

After centuries of continuous habitation in Asia Minor, indigenous Armenian, Greek, and Syriac Christians were forcibly removed by Ottoman authorities under the cover of the First World War. As a result, only a few small pockets of these communities exist in their ancestral homeland today.

The attack on communities that had survived and even thrived for centuries under Ottoman rule has been analyzed by historians and mourned by survivor communities living in exile. The Ottoman Armenian community, in particular, was the target of a series of unprecedented convulsive episodes of Ottoman state violence inspired by new identity formations, including the introduction of liberal notions of equality and state centralization. The infusion of these new ways of governing, acquired from Europe, clashed with tradition and disrupted the ordinary daily business of the empire. Marginalized communities were anxious to secure their rights as equal citizens with constitutional protections, while Muslims grew resentful that the status quo had changed.

This era of reforms and state centralization subjected Armenians to centralized tax burdens on top of traditional taxes customarily offered in the form of winter lodging to Kurds in the eastern provinces.[1] While the state eliminated these traditions, Kurds continued to demand them as a right, redoubling the financial burdens on Armenians. Denying these privileges resulted in indignities that left Armenians with little to no recourse.

Armenians were not passive victims in the face of these predatory practices and resisted persecution. For example, when a fourteen-year-old Armenian girl, Gülizar, was kidnapped, raped, and held captive by a Kurdish notable, Musa Bey, a war between Armenian self-defense bands and those aligned with

---

[1] Donald Bloxham, *The Great Game of Genocide: Imperialism, Nationalism, and the Destruction of the Ottoman Armenians* (Oxford: Oxford University Press, 2007), 39–42 and Taner Akçam, *A Shameful Act: The Armenian Genocide and the Question of Turkish Responsibility* (New York: Metropolitan Books, 2006), 40–1.

her kidnapper broke out in 1889.[2] As the community attempted to use the mechanisms of the state to release her from captivity, even staging protests in the Ottoman capital, Gülizar miraculously freed herself. Historian Owen Robert Miller has argued that the high-profile kidnapping that made waves at both the local and international scales gave birth to the Armenian *fedayi* or resistance movement.[3] The kidnapping of Gülizar, however, only foreshadowed more anti-Armenian violence on the horizon.

Repeated and patterned mass violence was amplified during the Hamidiye Massacres (1894–6), when Armenian communities in the eastern provinces of the empire were assaulted by Kurdish "Hamidiye" forces aligned with Ottoman Sultan Abdul Hamid II (r. 1876–1909). The Ottoman Sultan, in his effort to unify the empire, instrumentalized Islam to unify Muslims across ethnicities, isolating his non-Muslim subjects. Abdul Hamid's divide-and-rule policy terrorized Armenians in the imperial capitol and in the villages and towns where they were plundered and raped. Kurdish forces who murdered 100,000 to 300,000 Armenians were rewarded with privileges for their loyalty to the empire with the spoils of war (land and revenue).[4] These catastrophic moments of government repression not only resumed earlier efforts for a constitutional revolution but also stirred Armenian nationalist imaginaries in the late Ottoman Empire. The desire for revolutionary change was shared by Turkish and non-Turkish subjects in many parts of the empire, inspired by ideas of modernity and progress acquired from Europe.

Moving forward to 1908, the political climate had changed considerably. Armenians were elated by the success of the Committee of Union and Progress. Reflective of the tragic hopefulness of this moment, Armenians extended invitations to Ottoman officials to celebrate the revolution with Armenians and other minoritized groups with a mass at the Armenian Church of Yerortutiun (Holy Trinity) in Pera. The revolutionary ambience of the moment enhanced the common sentiment that equality would be secured under a common constitution, allowing the empire, in its new secular iteration, to cohere.[5] This euphoria was, however, short-lived. The fleeting excitement of the revolution rekindled ethno-religious animosities unleashed decades before. A year later,

---

[2] Arménouhie Kévonian, *Les Noces Noires de Gulizar* (Marseilles: Edition Parenthèses, 2005).
[3] Robert Owen Miller, "Back to the Homeland (*Tebi Yergir*): Or, how Peasants became Revolutionaries in Muş," *Journal of the Ottoman and Turkish Studies Association* 4, no. 2 (2017): 287–308. The term *fedayi* is derived from the Arabic *fida'i* which means "one who sacrifices" (for the homeland).
[4] Akçam, *A Shameful Act*, 46.
[5] Bedross Der Matossian, *Shattered Dreams of Empire: From Liberty to Violence in the Late Ottoman Empire* (Stanford: Stanford University Press, 2014), 23–4.

on April 13, 1909, reactionary Islamists aligned with Sultan Abdul Hamid attempted a counterrevolutionary coup d'état. While the counterrevolutionary movement was centered in Istanbul, it was reflective of Muslim political and economic resentments reverberating throughout the empire. That very month, the tide of sectarianism swelled throughout the realm, touching down in the Ottoman province of Adana.

The assault on Adana (1909) would claim 20,000 lives and raze half the Cilician city known for its economic vitality. In his recent analysis of the Adana Massacres, Bedross Der Matossian illustrates how political violence was produced by complex socioeconomic and political developments in the late Ottoman Empire.[6] Fueled by an emerging public sphere, the 1908 revolution had the dual effect of mobilizing not only positive sentiments but also negative ones that ossified religious identities. But underlying the events was economic resentment toward the prosperous Christian bourgeoisie that dominated the region's cotton industry: the Armenians, and often overlooked victims, Greeks, Assyrians, and Chaldeans.

As sectarian violence erupted in Adana, the Armenians protected themselves with self-defense bands that were understood by the government and Muslim locals as an Armenian uprising.[7] Armenians in places like Hadjin and Dörtyol, for instance, had fought in successful self-defense campaigns while others deployed non-violent "humanitarian resistance" in the form of medical, educational, and other humanitarian aid. Armenians would organize their own relief efforts again in 1915.[8] Armenian women were noteworthy humanitarians, among them Armenian feminists Zabel Yesayan (1879–1943) and Arshaguhi Teotig (1875–1922). Both activist writers devoted themselves to documenting the atrocities committed in Adana and the Armenian resistance to it.[9] Adana was, however, a sentinel foretelling even worse catastrophes on the horizon. By 1913, a counterrevolutionary triumvirate would seize control of the empire and implement a program of demographic engineering to transform a diverse, multireligious, multiethnic empire into an exclusively Turkish modern nation-

---

[6] Bedross Der Matossian, *Horrors of Adana: Revolution and Violence in the Early Twentieth Century* (Stanford: Stanford University Press, 2022), 3–9.
[7] Der Matossian, *Horrors of Adana*, 97–8.
[8] Khatchig Mouradian, *The Resistance Network: The Armenian Genocide and Humanitarianism in Ottoman Syria, 1915-1918* (Lansing: Michigan State University Press, 2021).
[9] See Zabel Essayan, Աւերակներու Մէջ *[Among the Ruins]* (Istanbul: Aras, 2010, 2011) translated as Zabel Essayan's *In the Ruins: The 1909 Massacres of Armenians in Adana, Turkey*, trans. G.M. Goshgarian, ed. Judith Saryan, Danila Jebejian Terpanjian, and Joy Renjilian-Burgy (Boston: AIWA Press, 2016). Translated into Turkish as *Yıkıntılar Arasında*, trans. Kayuş Çalıkman Gavrilof, ed. Ardaşes Margosyan (Istanbul: Aras, 2014). And Arshaguhi Teotig, Ամիս մը ի Կիլիկիա [A Month in Cilicia] (Constantinople: V & H. Der Nersesian, 1910).

state. The revolutionary triumvirate of "Young Turks" consisted of three figures whose names continue to horrify their victims: Talaat Pasha, Enver Pasha, and Cemal Pasha.[10]

When the triumvirate ascended, more fuel was doused on the fire of sectarian violence. During the Balkan Wars (1912–13), Muslim refugees (*muhacirler*) flooded into the peninsula carrying with them stories of murder and mayhem, which intensified Muslim animosity against Christians in Ottoman lands.[11] In the minds of Muslim victims from the Balkans, European and Near Eastern Christians were a homogeneous collective Christian perpetrator. The Balkan atrocities upset the natural order of Muslim supremacy embedded in the Ottoman political and social hierarchies. These stories of oppression along with the outbreak of the First World War and a humiliating Ottoman defeat on the Russian border motivated Ottoman soldiers to begin attacking Armenians. The empire identified its own Christian Greek and Armenian populations as "fifth columns," clandestine enemy agents working in collaboration with the Allied powers.

After assuming power, Young Turk theoreticians began articulating the idea of a unitary Turkish homeland that, though framed as secular, retained the notion that Turkishness was partially defined by a Muslim religious identity.[12] Emerging ethnonationalist ideology was disseminated throughout Asia Minor/Anatolia in pamphlets, journals, plays, correspondence, and speeches.[13] In 1914, the junta first set its aim on deporting an estimated 2 million Greeks from the Western and Black Sea (Pontic) regions murdering an estimated 300,000 to 1.5 million

---

[10] Of course, these names do not horrify elements of the population who were unaffected by their policies. In the Arab World, Cemal Pasha is notorious for his violent suppression of Arab nationalists in Lebanon and Syria, including mass executions in public squares in Beirut and Damascus. He is also remembered for the Aintoura Orphanage where Armenian and Kurdish children were forcibly assimilated into Muslim Turks. There has been an effort to revive Cemal Pasha's image as a benevolent humanitarian in Turkish scholarship. See Karnig Panian, *Goodbye Aintoura: A Memoir of the Armenian Genocide* (Stanford: Stanford University Press, 2015) and Ümit Kurt, "A Rescuer, an Enigma and a Génocidaire: Cemal Pasha," *The End of the Ottomans: The Genocide of 1915 and the Politics of Turkish Nationalism*, ed. Hans-Lukas Kieser, Margaret Lavinia Anderson, Seyhan Bayraktar, and Thomas Schmutz (London: Bloomsbury, 2019), 221–45.

[11] Doğan Çetinkaya, "'Revenge! Revenge! Revenge!' 'Awakening a Nation' Through Propaganda in the Ottoman Empire during the Balkan Wars (1912–1913)," in *World War I and the End of the Ottomans: From the Balkan Wars to the Armenian Genocide*, ed. Hans-Lukas Kieser, Kerem Öktem, and Maurus Reinkowski (London: Bloomsbury, 2015), 85.

[12] This nationalist agenda which merged Turkishness with Muslim identity would later be articulated in secular Kemalist education as "We are a Turkish race, of Turkish blood, of Muslim faith," see Jenny White, *Muslim Nationalism and the New Turks* (Princeton: Princeton University Press, 2012), 6.

[13] Two figures, Mehmed Ziyâ Gökalp (1876–1924) and the historian Yusuf Akçura (1876–1935), were pivotal in constructing emerging Turkish ethnonationalism. Ryan Gingeras, *Fall of the Sultanate: The Great War and the End of the Ottoman Empire 1908-1922* (Oxford: Oxford University Press, 2016), 110–16.

people.[14] The 1914 deportations would be followed up with Greek-Turkish population exchanges at war's end. The formula for Greeks—conscription of males in unarmed labor battalions and the mass deportation of the general population—would be deployed against the Armenians the following year.

The Ottoman assault on Armenians in 1915 was far more systematic and organized than it was in the previous century. After the arrest of 250 Armenian intellectuals and politicians on April 24, 1915, the Ottomans issued the *Sevk ve İskân Kanunu* (Relocation and Resettlement Law), which would systematically pluck the historic Armenian community from its homeland. The law claimed that Armenians would be "relocated" in the Syrian Desert, a space government officials considered a wasteland full of "wild tribes" (*aşair-i mutavahhişe*). The "desert province" was, in their view, an ideal space to disappear segments of the population that stood in the way of Turkish biopolitics.[15] Deportation (*tehcir*) was code for murder since many Armenians never left the threshold of their homes nor the boundaries of their villages and cities. While it was publicly declared a necessity for national security against insurrectionist Armenians, the genocidal campaign moved beyond military objectives to deracinate Armenians from the Anatolian landscape.

Reflective of the late Ottoman biopolitical state, the Armenian Genocide was a murder by numbers designed with the assistance of modern social science, methods captured in architect Talaat Pasha's black book that meticulously logged pre- and post-genocide Armenian population statistics.[16] The demographic engineering of the population targeted groups deemed non-assimilable to the emerging Turkish national identity—Greeks, Armenians, Assyrians, and the Kurdish population, the latter of which was targeted as early as 1916.[17]

While historians had previously dated the Armenian Genocide from 1915 to 1919, some historians include the Greek–Turkish population exchanges that

---

[14] Benny Morris and Dror Ze'evi summarize demographic projections on the Greek population as follows: the League of Nations estimated there were 2 million Greeks in Asia Minor prior to deportation and a conservative projection of casualties is 300,000 from historian Justin McCarthy and the larger figure of 1.5 million deaths from historian Tessa Hofmann. See *The Thirty-Year Genocide: Turkey's Destruction of Its Christian Minorities, 1894-1924* (Cambridge, MA: Harvard University Press, 2019), 487.

[15] Of course, the region of Dayr al-Zur, populated by Arab Bedouin, was hardly a wasteland. See Fuat Dündar, *Crime of Numbers: The Role of Statistics in the Armenian Question (1878-1918)* (New York: Transaction, 2010), 77–8 and Samuel Dolbee, *Locusts of Power: Borders, Empire, and Environment in the Modern Middle East* (Cambridge: Cambridge University Press, 2023), 62.

[16] Dündar, *Crime of Numbers*, 103–22 and Talat Paşa'nın, *Evrak-ı Metrukesi: Sadrazam Talat Paşa'nın özel arşivinde bulunan Ermeni tehciri konuşundaki belgeler ve hususi yazışmalar*, ed. Murat Bardakçı (Istanbul: Everest Yayinlari, 2008).

[17] Uğur Ümit Üngör, *The Making of Modern Turkey: Nation and State in Eastern Anatolia, 1913-1950* (Oxford: Oxford University Press, 2011), 30–2.

forcibly deported over 1.5 million people under League of Nations supervision and the Lausanne Treaty (1923). Today, many signs of Armenian existence in Anatolia since recorded history have disappeared, and the abandoned rubble of Greek villages on the Mediterranean coast is barely recognized by tourists as the remnants of this violent undoing.

The Ottoman state committed genocide under the cover of war as nationalist sentiments were inflamed on the battlefield exacerbating Christian xenophobia. Historian Uğur Ümit Üngör perhaps captured the historical moment best when he wrote: "No matter how much difficulty the Young Turks had in defining what 'Turkishness' was, it took them only a few years to define what Turkishness was not."[18] The role of *ressentiment*—the powerful emotion of resentment and a desire for revenge against the Other—in forging modern national identities, as well as populist-authoritarian social mobilization, cannot be underestimated.[19] The emerging ethnonationalist state defined itself against its enemies during wartime, excluding non-Muslim Christian communities deemed agents of Western (i.e., Christian) imperialism. Armenians had developed sophisticated political parties, but upon closer examination, many of them were engaged with the Ottoman state, even serving in the Ottoman parliament until the state adopted its eliminationist final solution.

It is within this broader historical context of war and genocide that Armenian feminist, educator, and writer Zabel Yesayan bore witness to Haig Toroyan's testimony. The arc of Zabel's life follows the pattern of the three major catastrophic episodes of late Ottoman, anti-Armenian state violence. Being the only woman intellectual on the list of over 250 Armenians arrested on "Red Sunday," April 24, 1915, she fled the empire and eventually penned many of her essays, reports, and testimonies from abroad.[20] *The Agony of a People* is just one example of the public lectures and reports that she compiled in Paris while in exile.[21] Importantly, Zabel, like many other Armenian intellectuals during and

---

[18] Üngör, *The Making of Modern Turkey*, 52.
[19] *Ressentiment*, a concept that originates with Friedrich Nietzsche, is not itself an analytic, but the concept can be a tool to access deeper political and emotional drivers that motivate the politics of regression and the desire for revenge against cultural others. See Rahel Jaeggi, "Modes of Regression: The Case of Ressentiment," *Critical Times* 5, no. 3 (2022): 501–37.
[20] Of those politicians, activists, lawyers, doctors, journalists, and artists arrested, 174 were executed by the Ottoman state. See Lerna Ekmekcioglu, *Recovering Armenia: The Limits of Belonging in Post-Genocide Turkey* (Stanford: Stanford University Press, 2016), 4.
[21] Zabel composed many speeches and reports that build upon one another. Two important ones are a report she composed for the Armenian National Committee for use at the Paris Peace Conference, Zabel Yesayan, "La libération des Femmes et Enfants Non-musulmans en Turquie," *Th/e March 1919 Report*, 1–15, Correspondence February–March 1919, *Nubarian* Library, Armenian National Delegation Archives, 1–11 and a speech at the Sorbonne on January 17, 1920, titled "Le role de la femme Arménienne pendant la guerre," *La Revue des études arméniennes* 2 (1922): 121–38.

after the genocide, set about compiling and documenting survivor testimony using her literary talent to document the voices of women and children in 1909 and again in 1915. In *Agony of a People*, she amplifies survivor Haig Toroyan's voice as well as those who likely did not survive the carnage but whose stories were preserved in his own memory. Zabel miraculously conjures the ghosts of those Armenian martyrs and gives them the power to speak beyond the grave in a first-person narration. Yesayan's compilation of Toroyan's testimony in the summer of 1916 echoes over a century of Armenian historical, ethnographic, artistic, and literary work that archives the truth of 1915 in a climate of genocide denial and state-orchestrated erasure.

Born in 1892 in Aleppo, Toroyan was living in Diyarbakir when the massacre of the local Armenian and Assyrian population was set into motion by the Ottoman authorities. His unique story of survival details the trials and tribulations of Armenian deportees and the everyday resistance they deployed to survive unthinkable horrors. Toroyan witnesses the remnants of his nation floating down the Euphrates River and the rape and plunder they suffered as they were preyed upon during deportations. Inside the caravans of Armenian deportees in Jarablus (Syria), Toroyan documents his efforts sheltering and rescuing Armenians from the precipice of death. At one point, he cunningly disguises himself as a translator for the Germans and smuggles bread to starving Armenian deportees resisting the forces of death. Having provided Yesayan with his eyewitness testimony, *Agony of a People* offers us an on-the-ground perspective of the Armenian Genocide a year into the extermination process. At war's end, Toroyan returned to Aleppo to assist his people only to return to Tehran where he would live for twenty-five years. Later in life, he returned to Aleppo to live out his final days with his brother.

Narrating in 1916, Toroyan could not have predicted that after the organized slaughter of 1 million Ottoman Armenians the crime would continue to be denied by the state of Turkey. The burden of history has been placed on the survivor community. Zabel's transcription of survivor testimony should be placed within the broader context of Armenian Genocide acknowledgment within a climate of denial. Armenians were and continue to be a unique existential enemy, captured in the ease through which Turkish nationalists upon hearing the word "Armenian" (*ermeni*) offer the accompanying "betrayers of the homeland" (*vatan hainleri*). More than the Greeks, whose ancient rootedness and longevity have been long forgotten by the modern state of Turkey, the Armenian, even in her absence, remains a threat to national security, with resistance and survival seen as a national betrayal.

Note on Transliteration

Words and place-names in Armenian are rendered in English according to the Library of Congress transliteration system for Western Armenian. Throughout the text, Yesayan's use of Armenian names for places is maintained, while their modern Turkish equivalents are also provided. Words in Arabic and Ottoman Turkish are rendered according to the IJMES transliteration system.

Dr. Maral Aktokmakyan and Dr. Tamar M. Boyadjian

Introduction by Zabel Yesayan from Original Publication in Korz, February and March 1917, Baku

The painful duty has fallen to me, to set down in writing, the images and impressions seen and borne by the only eyewitness to the Armenian people dying in Mesopotamia, Mr. Haig Toroyan. A sole Armenian who, by virtue of his vigilance and steadfastness traversing those cruel exilic roads, has arrived here to transmit and bear witness to the plaintive cries released by an entire people dying in the Mesopotamian deserts.

It is not the result of chance, nor were ordinary virtues and qualities enough for that one Armenian to have the ability to fulfill his role. He felt his obligation as a sacred one; and imbued with that feeling, approached all the scattered groups, listened to all the sounds of suffering, saw the hideous in all its unspeakable images; and, crossing the Turkish border, impassable for an Armenian, arrived to us, bringing with him the ultimate cry of a people being annihilated in an indescribable horror.

It is difficult to approach such a dreadful topic, difficult to mentally live through those periods of agony collectively experienced by flocks of Armenians, who were subjected to the cruel and implacable executioners' sneers, insults, and all ranges of dishonor.

Painfully imbued with the part of the duty that had fallen upon me, I considered it sacrilege to turn an entire people's pangs of death into a work of literature; to turn to literature the unspeakable story of the violation of maidens, of the fragments of a civilized nation dehumanized by pain and misery; of crowds dying from thirst on riverbanks even as they stared at running water; of spirits still living in mounds of corpses, of martyred children; of educated girls and wives turned into commodities to be bought and sold, and of mothers in throes. And this is why I approached this work with the utmost sincerity and respect.

What the Armenian or foreign reader will find in this account goes above and beyond the most infernal fancy. It is undoubtedly the case that, in these universal horrors of war, when in all corners of the world human feelings have been blunted by the shock occasioned by everyday miseries, the Armenian people's suffering nevertheless has the particularity to astonish all humanity and, with horror and dread, to move its conscience.

Only the Turk could have enjoyed primacy in these bloody years because crime is the only thing at which they could have remained unrivalled. Crime, with all its horrid zeniths and hellish delicacies, is the only cultivated and perfected capability to which that wretched stock gives fruit, as the product of its nation's spirit.

Humanity's strictest measure of justice is incapable of judging, nor can it even come close to comprehending those evils to which the Turks subjected a guiltless and defenseless population. But at the same time, I am convinced that even the enormity and improbability of those crimes will leave them unpunished.

Years pass by, and political resentments and enmities are forgotten. A new era of humanity, with its new hopes and inclinations, forgets today's mourning and misery; however, something will remain irremediable and unforgettable, and that is an entire people's protracted and tormenting agony, one portrait of which, discolored as it may be, you will find in the following pages.

1

Dikranagerd, November 1914. Economic Boycott. The Burning of the Bazaar. Military Requisitions and Mobilization.[1]

In November 1914, I was in Dikranagerd (for the business of) buying antiques.[2] This was the state of the city before the final catastrophes. Half of Dikranagerd's inhabitants are Armenian, and the other half are made up of Turks and Kurds. Among the Armenians, moreover, there is a small number of Assyrians who are Armenian speakers, just as one portion of the Turks and Kurds speak Armenian. The Armenians have four national schools, two churches, and a prelacy. The city's Armenians are primarily merchants and artisans. Dikranagerd has become the commercial center of the north-eastern provinces; and the goods from these provinces—namely, wheat, oil, sheep, wool, gum, silk, and silk fabrics—converge here to be exported elsewhere. The Armenians of Dikranagerd had an irrigation system and printing houses, in addition to numerous factories for manufacturing flour, silk cloths, and cigar papers. Only one flour mill in Dikranagerd belonged to a Turk, namely the city's Turkish deputy.

After the proclamation of the Constitution,[3] Dikranagerd's Armenian villages also experienced a period of prosperity. The Armenians repurchased those lands they had lost under the despotic regime, and having acquired agricultural machines in addition to following new agricultural methods, they quickly began to grow wealthy. Even those Turks considered affluent, but especially the Kurds, who make up a considerable majority of the Muslim population, were at the service of the Armenians. Since Armenians had money and influence, they were also entrusted with contract work.

---

[1] [Zabel Yesayan, appearing hereafter as ZY] The following pages are written in the first person, because they are Mr. Toroyan's oral descriptions and impressions, which I have written down.
[2] [Editors' Note: Dr. Maral Aktokmakyan and Dr. Tamar M. Boyadjian, appearing hereafter as MA, TMB]: present-day Diyarbakır, Turkey.
[3] [Translator's Note: Arakel Minassian, appearing hereafter as AM]: A reference to the reestablishment of the Ottoman Constitution, a result of the Young Turk revolution of 1908.

This economic flourishing was accompanied by a significant improvement in the intellectual life of the Dikranagerd Armenians. They built libraries and a theater and organized an orchestra. As in all places inhabited by Armenians, here too the Armenian people embraced the work of their rebirth with great ardour and haste, bringing forth such an ebullient public life, which was in many ways distant and different from the slow and backward life of those in power. The Armenians' superiority, under a free and liberal regime, manifested itself so clearly, that the Muslim residents, willingly or unwillingly, submitted to that superiority. For instance, when a dispute broke out between Armenian and Turkish or Kurdish villagers, both sides eagerly deferred to councils made up of Armenians, which would settle the dispute justly and impartially, often playing a conciliatory role. As tired as they were of the slow and corrupt Turkish courts, sometimes the Muslims submitted to these councils even when the dispute was among themselves.

In this state of affairs, it was impossible for the Turkish people to compete with the Armenians' expanding progress. The Ittihadists[4] were especially worried, and knowing it to be practically impossible to put their paralytic population in motion, they began resorting directly to government measures to counteract the influence of Armenians. The fight began in the terrain of economics: taking advantage of the economic boycott of Christians, which had been proclaimed as a result of the Balkan War, the Ittihadists began agitating among the Muslim inhabitants and at the same time established a store by the name of *Islamic Shop* [*Maghazayi islamie*], which sold all kinds of products. Both openly and secretly, they exhorted the Muslims to cut off all ties with Armenians and to buy goods only from other Muslims, especially from that store established by the Ittihadists. Through government intercession, they opened lines of credit for Turkish landholders, and the agricultural bank dedicated its resources solely to Muslim villagers. The Armenians sensed the meaning of this feverish activity, but remained calm. The bazaar was in their hands, and they competed peacefully with the Ittihadists, as their European goods, which were diverse, high-quality, and even affordable, were enough to maintain their clientele. The store known as *Maghazayi islamie* remained stagnant, and the Ittihadists' agitations proved ineffective in delivering serious harm to the economic progress of the Armenians. The Ittihadist government sought new opportunities to ruin the

---

[4] [MA, TMB] also known as the Unionists, they were the members of the nationalist political organization, Committee of Union and Progress (CUP) which played a vital role in a wide range of events from the dethronement of Sultan Hamid, and the reestablishment of the Ottoman Constitution, to the Cilician massacres, ruling the Ottoman Empire from 1913 to 1918.

Armenian market; and to this end, they even published a local newspaper,[5] whose typesetters and printers, however, they were forced to pick from among the Armenians.

Bearing all this in mind, it is very easy to imagine what a terrific opportunity these mobilizations and military requisitions offered the government—a chance to lawfully plunder the Armenians. The Ittihadist chief Memduh Bey and a representative from the army personally carried out the requisitions. They entered the Armenian shops in the market and subjected them to plunder, almost without exception or restraint. They confiscated all kinds of goods, even those which could in no way serve military efforts. The military, moreover, had the Armenian tailors, whom they worked as soldiers without pay, use the requisitioned wool to make clothes for their wives and children.

Dikranagerd's Armenian villages were also subject to the same harassment. The military requisitioned almost everything: merchandise, provisions, carriages, and all kinds of animals.

In the middle of a November night, with everything having been confiscated on the pretext of military need, the Armenian market was burned down at the hands of the Ittihadist police and night watchmen. The market was connected on one side to the Turkish market and districts, but when the fire reached that point, the government used every means necessary to halt the fire's progress.

On the day before the fire, the government had assembled 4,000 to 5,000 Kurds from the surrounding villages under the pretense of military service; then, they released them one day after the fire. It was clear that this had all been organized in advance. If the Armenians were to make any serious effort to put out the fire, or to overcome the governmental obstacles to doing so, those Kurds would have been released to massacre and plunder the Armenians.

And as mentioned, while the fire raged, the government used all the means necessary to stop the Armenians from putting it out and saving their wares. They did not allow a single person to approach the site of the catastrophe; the police and gendarmes[6] had surrounded the market and did not even make a show of assistance. The fire progressively spread, and the Armenian people feared that it would reach their districts. They also feared the church was in danger. All the young men were away, as they had been drafted into military service. But

---

[5] [ZY] The issues of those local Turkish newspapers are considerably useful and represent proof of the Turks' premeditated criminality. Obtaining these collections must be one of our primary concerns.
[6] [MA, TMB] The Ottoman Gendarmerie, also known as zaptı, was a paramilitary police organization of the nineteenth century Ottoman Empire. Among other military forces, the gendarmerie gradually became the principal security and defense force of the empire, which occurred during the reforms of the Tanzimat era (1839–76).

one group, including women and girls, began working furiously to save the Armenian quarters and the church. In a similar vein, they tried to demolish Mardiros Atarian's silk factory. And the Turkish soldiers—instead of helping and calling in the firefighters—became obstacles instead, ridiculing the Armenians.

> That's enough, what are you doing? they said. What's going on that you're choking us in dust like this?

The fire consumed 1,143 shops, including 7 bakeries, 3 caravanserais, and a few coffeehouses. The Armenians' material losses were considerable. To give a sense of the fire's effects, it is worth recalling that 500,000 *liras*[7] were imperiled, which had been lent to the Dikranagerd Armenians by those in Aleppo. In a flash, Armenian commerce was nearly ruined, especially since, not only was there no means of recovery, but on the contrary, the government put every means in motion to complete the Armenians' economic destruction.

The municipal courts were closed due to the mobilization, so when Turkish and Kurdish debtors refused to pay their debts to the Armenians, the latter had no means of enforcing their rights.

Directly after the fire, the government announced the conscription of all men under forty-five years old to be completed within three days. The Armenians began to sell or stake their homes in haste and practically gave away their finery in order to pay the *bedel*[8] that exempted them from military service—which for various reasons they considered extremely dangerous, especially as Armenians. It was by these desperate measures that one large portion of those destined for the army were saved. But the value of all Armenian goods had fallen. The government would not accept five lira coins, which the women used to ornament themselves with. And so, the Armenians were forced to sell directly to the Turkish people, who bought the coins for three and a half liras. Silk was sold at half price, and a five- to six-room house was sold at sixty to seventy liras.

After squeezing out every last ounce of their strength, the government declared that the Armenians were to hand over their copper dishes, tents, beds, and other materials for the soldiers. Whoever had these items hastened to hand them over, because the military authorities resorted to all manners of violence. Under the pretense of inspection, the gendarmes entered their homes, searching and plundering them. They carried away everything they could find: provisions, copperware, and (in place of tents) expensive carpets and linens.

---

[7] [AM] the Ottoman pound. Today, the Turkish lira is worth 100 kuruş, but the exchange rate was more variable in the Ottoman Empire.
[8] [AM] Payment given as exemption from military service.

After burning down the market, the Turks further attempted to set fire to the Armenian quarters, but the Armenian night watchmen caught the arsonists, and the danger was thus averted.

Government pressure progressively became unbearable—as both moral and material blows rained down on the Armenian population without respite. On the pretext of looking for arms, the government searched the church with a mob of 150–200 Turks and Kurds. They sought any reason whatsoever to plunder and destroy, but their search was fruitless. Returning empty-handed, the rabble came across an elderly priest, and every one of its members struck a blow onto the poor man's head, beating him to death.

At around the same time, Armenian deputy to the Ottoman Parliament Stepan Chrajian *Effendi* and his two sons, who were likewise government officials, were hanged for the sole reason that their family was considered *Hnchakian*.[9]

Seeing the government's hostile position, it is natural that many of the Armenians did not present themselves for conscription. But in place of the deserter, the Turks would imprison a father, a mother, or a sister, until the young man finally came forward to save his family.

In the month of November, the Birecik[10] fire took place. There, too, the market was burned down, and seventy stores were destroyed, along with many houses. News of similar incidents from various Armenian-inhabited areas left no doubt as to the Turks' intentions, and all were seized with heavy disquiet.

Shortly before my departure, the Ottoman Bank declared in nearly all its local branches—including the ones in Dikranagerd, Aleppo, and Bitlis—that those who owed money to the bank needed to pay those debts within a specific timeframe. The bank would confiscate the immovable assets of those who could not pay, and the debtors would be declared bankrupt. Those who had set money aside in the bank, moreover, were forbidden from collecting it. This unjust ordinance resulted in many Armenians being declared bankrupt and becoming subject to all the particular misfortunes of that condition.

The Armenian people knew very well how high the Turks' hatred could rise, even though high-ranking officials used cunning tactics to cloak their intentions. In Dikranagerd, as in all other places, the enemy conducted themselves

---

[9] [AM] Members of the Social Democratic *Hnchak* [Bell] Party, a revolutionary Armenian party founded in 1887 in Geneva, Switzerland, with the goal of establishing an independent socialist Armenia. Chrajian and his sons were arrested on April 21, along with several other notables, and were tortured. Stepan Chrajian was not hanged, but was among the last notables killed outside the city on June 9. See Raymond Kevorkian, *The Armenian Genocide: A Complete History* (London: I.B. Tauris, 2011), 361–2.

[10] [ZY] Birecik is a town on the shore of the Euphrates, 100 kilometers south of Aleppo. [MA, TMB] Currently the district is part of the city Urfa in modern-day Turkey.

skillfully. Having gradually pressured and plucked off, piece by piece, material and spiritual strengths of the Armenian people, [the enemy] subjected them to ultimate annihilation when there was no longer any chance of resistance. The Dikranagerd Armenians possessed enough guns, but would not dare to resort to violent means, since the strongest among them were away on military duty. One part of the population suggested resisting and taking refuge on the Sasun mountains. But, the absence of young men, the lack of organization, and the lingering hope that anything—at least a portion of the Armenians—could be saved, rendered the majority cautious and anxious, while the elderly made desperate efforts to appease the government.

Their hopes came to nothing, and their prudence was fruitless. The Turkish government had ample time to carry out its plan, and in the end, the Armenian people of Dikranagerd were subjected to deportation and extermination.

2

Jarābulus, December 1914 to November 12, 1915. The Condition of the Armenians Until February 1915. The First Signs of Enmity. The Attempt to Massacre 2,000 Armenian Workers. The Incident of the Loggers.

I left Dikranagerd toward the end of November 1914 and traveled southwest through Siverek,[1] where the mobilization and military requisitions had been carried out with the same injustice and cruelty as in Dikranagerd. The local doctors, who were all Armenian, had answered the government's call—regardless of their age—and were working fervently and tirelessly for the military. That very same government oppressed not only the general Armenian population but also those same doctors' families. A gloomy and hopeless sadness had come over everyone, and they already sensed what a terrible end awaited them.

From Siverek, I made my way to Edessa (Urfa), where the situation was more peaceful at that time. I hastened on to Jarābulus, and having traveled for four days by cart from Dikranagerd to Arap Punar and then two hours by train, I arrived in Jarābulus within five days.

Jarābulus is a town a hundred kilometers from Aleppo, on the bank of the Euphrates, and, as such, one of the important stops on the Baghdad railway. This area is entirely Arab, and the Armenians make up an insignificant minority; since there are only a few Turks, the Armenians' situation is quite calm. Even in the most bitter days, and compared [with other places], the situation here was bearable. When I arrived in Jarābulus, the Arabs and Turks were on friendly terms with the Armenians and protested in astonishment while speaking about the events that had taken place in other regions.

Are we not brothers, children of the same fatherland? they would say.

---

[1] [MA, TMB] Now a district in Urfa, Turkey. The name of this place derives from Armenian and means "black ruins" (from Armenian *uku* "black" and *աւերակ* "ruins").

The mobilization and military requisitions had taken place within the bounds of the law, and as such, it was impossible to compare the condition of these Armenians with those in Dikranagerd. There were Armenians among the government officials, and the confiscated goods were handed over to an Armenian. Although all the non-Muslim schools were commandeered for the soldiers, only the Armenian school was left alone. This somewhat good situation lasted until February 1915.

One of my Turkish friends, with whom I was close, had been in Aleppo. He returned while I was in Jarābulus, and I went to visit him.

Welcome back, I said happily.

He looked at me sternly and sadly and showed no sign of friendship, as if I were a complete stranger.

Welcome back, I repeated, confused by his manner.

No, keep your greeting to yourself, he replied dryly. There's no more friendship between us: it's all finished.

Why? I asked.

I can't tell you right now. You'll find out some day.

In those days, we observed some irritation among the Turks. Gathered in the coffeehouses, they spoke in hushed tones; and whenever an Armenian appeared, they fell silent. Strange reports circulated about Armenian revolts and the insults and sufferings borne by Turkish women and children. There was no doubt in our minds that this was the result of intentional and organized agitation among the Muslim inhabitants, with the purpose of turning them against the Armenians.

In the first days of February, in 1915, as whispers of hostile acts were spreading among our region's Muslim inhabitants, a crowd of Armenian workers poured into Jarābulus: half-dead, frightened, and practically naked. As they explained what happened to them, they beseeched the local Armenians for help.

Here is what happened:

Between Resulayn[2] and Mdzpin[3] was a German construction site where about 2,000 Armenian laborers, associated with the railroad, worked. The soldier in charge of the site's defense goes with his gendarmes to gather the surrounding Chechens and Circassians, and they rush to the camp and force the Armenian

---

[2] [MA, TMB] also known as Raʾs al-ʿAyn, is one of the oldest cities in Upper Mesopotamia. It is also known as the ancient Aramean city of Sikkan, the Roman city of Rhesaina, and the Byzantine city of Theodosiopolis. Currently in the Al-Ḥasakah Governorate, Raʾs al-ʿAyn is on the Syria-Turkey border.

[3] [MA, TMB] modern-day Nusaybin, a municipality and district of Mardin, Turkey.

workers to drop everything and follow them. Under close surveillance, they take the laborers to a nearby Circassian village, where they subject them to complete plunder. They strip them of everything they can find, even their clothes. Some are left with only their shirts, but most are stripped naked. After doing all this, they split the Armenians into groups of five and take the first group to a nearby hill. At the foot of the hill, those condemned to death see a large ditch has already been prepared for them. The Chechens and Circassians begin stabbing the Armenians one by one; by the time they killed the third person, out of nowhere, the Armenians' saviors arrive on the spot and stop the murderers.

Resulayn's surveyors and foremen—who were Greeks, Italians, and Armenians—upon hearing that a mob of Chechens and Circassians had taken their workers by force, marched straight to the local *kaymakam*,[4] who was asleep at the time. After waking him, they explain that if the workers are massacred, he will be the one to bear the heavy responsibility. They finally push him not only to promptly send help but also to join them in seeking out the victims. In this way, they arrive at the site of the massacre and free the nearly naked survivors from the hands of the Turkish soldier. When the *kaymakam* asks the soldier why he undertook such a cruel and foolish act, the soldier responds by handing him the order he had received by telegram.

The Armenian workers return with their liberators to the construction site, where their huts and tents are also found. They plan to take all their belongings and flee to Aleppo, but they immediately discover that everything has already been plundered.

As a result of the war, the German railroad used up all its coal; they become forced to burn wood to run their machines. Led by an Armenian, a group of Armenians and many Kurdish and Turkish workers assumed the task of procuring the necessary wood. A *kaymakam* and a group of gendarmes had joined them to protect the workers. They reach the monastery of the Holy Saviour, in the Karadagh forest, where they begin their work. On May 3, 1915, the surrounding Turks and Kurds descend upon the Armenians and begin slaughtering the workers with axes right in front of their fellow Muslims' eyes. Many Armenians are wounded, and some escape into the river. The assistant to the *kaymakam*, who was an Armenian *gendarme*, protests to the local government on behalf of

---

[4] [MA, TMB] from the Arabic qā'im maqām meaning "stand-in" or "deputy"; kaymakam was a title used by various officials of the Ottoman Empire, including viziers, governors of provincial divisions, and administrators of district divisions. In simple terms, this could be translated as "district governor."

the railroad company and demands that the responsible parties be punished. Not having enough forces at his disposal, the local governor appeals to the *kaymakam* of Adıyaman for aid. But the latter refuses with the following reply:

> I'm the one who released those Turks and Kurds onto the Armenians. I received the orders, in accordance with which I was forced to act. You will see that there are already no Armenians left in our town, and you must hand those who are still hidden over to me. It's been decided: the men will be massacred, and the women and children will be driven to Mesopotamia.

At that point, the *kaymakam* of Adıyaman realizes that his counterpart's companion is an Armenian and demands that he be handed over, threatening to detain him by force if necessary. Not wanting to surrender his friend, the *kaymakam* strives to convince the governor of Adıyaman to let him go. But the Governor refuses to hear any objections and responds to these entreaties by presenting his orders. They succeed with great difficulty in saving the Armenian, and he immediately flees toward Aleppo.

3

The Deportations in Cilicia

Zeytun, Dört-yol (Chork Marzvan). Hajin. Aintab.[1]

Jemal Pasha, the commander of the Syrian army (who became the governor of the Adana and Aleppo vilayets after the Adana massacres), writes a letter to Sahag, the Catholicos of Cilicia, and asks him to exhort his people to make themselves docile and obedient. He notes specifically the Armenians in Zeytun,[2] Hajn,[3] and Dört-yol[4]—whose resistance had disrupted the intentions of the government in the past. He advises the Catholicos to use every means necessary to ensure that those populations follow the military commands to the letter and are ready to obey even when the deportation order is given. In exchange, he promises help and protection for the deported people of Cilicia if the need arises.

Sahag Catholicos communicates Jemal Pasha's order to all the dioceses under his jurisdiction, and he sends clergymen specifically to Zeytun, Hajn, and Dört-yol to communicate the exceptional difficulties of this situation.

Zeytun—As a result of the military desertions, Zeytun's four city councilmen had been imprisoned, and Nazaret Chavush[5] (a popular hero) had been beaten to death in prison. His son and a few other deserters climb the mountain and

---

[1] [ZY]: Mr. Haig Toroyan has collected accurate information about the manner of deportation in each of those places, having met, one-by-one, with exiled families or individuals from the aforementioned areas while in Jarābulus. Not wanting to embellish his story with suppositions or exaggerated details, we record only what is absolutely true. That is why we have so little to say about comparably important areas, such as Zeytun and Deort-eol. Since Aintab is closer to Jarābulus, the confirmed information is more complete. (Z.E.)

[2] [MA, TMB] present-day Süleymanlı in Marash, Turkey. Armenian inhabitants of Zeytun date back to even before the early medieval period. They were known for their resistance against Ottoman forces and preserved an autonomy for some time due to their defensive position in the mountains.

[3] [MA, TMB] Located at the Taurus mountains, Hadjin is a district of the Adana province and known today as Saimbeyli. Hajin is one of the Cilician Armenian towns known with its resistance against Turkish onslaught in 1920.

[4] [MA, TMB] Dörtyol, literally meaning "four roads" or "crossroads" in Turkish, was one of the Armenian-populated towns in the Adana vilayet. The town is also known for its Armenian resistance movement during the Cilician massacres. Yesayan renders the Armenian with a dash as such Sṭoṇǰ-ṭoṇ. We have decided to maintain her form.

[5] Çavuş (or Chavush) is sergeant in Turkish.

refuse to be handed over to the authorities. The government frames the act of these few young people as an uprising of Zeytun and therefore begins harassing its citizens. The news reaches the deserters who—outraged at the harassment borne by their families—descend into the city, rush upon the prison, and free the four council members, at which point a skirmish takes place that sees no losses on either side. Terrified, the local government blows the incident out of proportion. And to justify their incompetence and their failure to defend the prison from the attackers, they submit to the central authorities and declare that Zeytun is in rebellion, that the Armenians have attacked the government, and that prompt aid is absolutely necessary. Three thousand cavalrymen depart immediately from Aleppo under the leadership of Fakhri Pasha. They are joined by reservists from Aintab and Marash, and an army totaling 10,000 marches on Zeytun. Meeting no resistance whatsoever, the forces calmly enter Zeytun and immediately seize 300 men under the age of 30 or younger, and drive them into the Hauran desert, near Damascus. According to Arab soldiers, all 300 of those men were killed in the desert. The remaining population of Zeytun was deported in groups. They were sent to Birecik, from there to Urfa, and finally to the Hauran, where they remained for a long time. In the Hauran, the deported people of Zeytun were placed under the watch of a Turkish serviceman who conducted himself with profound hatred toward those entrusted to his supervision. The Turkish serviceman would encourage his soldiers to take revenge on the women and girls, who had taken the lives of many Turkish soldiers.[6] Two surveyors who had passed through the Hauran told us about this dire situation. To honor the surveyors, the Turkish serviceman had sent them two Armenian girls from Zeytun as a gift.

During the deportation from Zeytun, the Armenians were not allowed to take any of their things with them, nor were they allowed to take any form of transportation. They had only the clothes on their backs and provisions for three or four days. Immediately after emptying Zeytun of the Armenians, the government populates the place with Rumelian Turkish refugees, who at once take ownership of the homes, property, and provisions of the those who have gone.

Dört-yol—The government accused the Dört-yol Armenians of communicating with English battleships; and on that pretext, they gathered the majority of the men and sent them away to fortify military positions, to dig

---

[6] [ZY] An allusion to the assault by the women and girls of Zeytun on the local barracks. They surprised the menacing army with hammers, axes, and so on, killing many of the soldiers.

trenches, and to perform other manual labor. In the meantime, the women and children were deported to Aleppo, where their situation was calm, especially since the men were allowed to join their families there once their work was finished. They occupied themselves in Aleppo with agriculture and minor trade.

Hajin—After deporting the Armenians from Zeytun, Fahri Pasha and his soldiers moved on to Hajin. Having seen the miseries faced by those deported from other places, the Armenians here did not immediately comply with the authorities but rather engaged in a more calm opposition. Each family remained shut up in in its home; the market and streets were deserted, and it was as if the government orders, called out by town criers, were being directed at an empty city. Not wanting to resort to violence, Fahri Pasha entered into negotiations with the local notables. He promised and assured them that the deportations were imperative to the war effort, and that the people would arrive unharmed at their destination. And so, he succeeded in convincing the notables to comply with the orders. The Armenian population of Hajin was relocated to the areas surrounding Aleppo.

Aintab[7]—Aintab is one of the most lively and flourishing cities in Cilicia. It has 70,000 residents, 10,000 of whom are Armenian, while the rest are Turkish and Kurdish. Immediately after the proclamation of the Ottoman Constitution, an education commission was created with the goal of establishing an institute of higher education supported financially by the Cilician Armenians. The Adana massacre became an obstacle to the enactment of this plan, but the people of Aintab used their own means to open a normal school, the purpose of which was to prepare schoolteachers. Although the Armenians of Aintab are generally Turkish speakers, they have a great love for education and their nation; and even older people strove to become Armenian speakers. They have ten co-ed schools, one orphanage, one trade school, and so on. They had opened separate auditoriums for men and women and organized a theater company. Being naturally gifted, they became advanced particularly in the musical arts.

Their love for education and their openness to civilization—qualities which are characteristic of their nature—turned Aintab into the educational center of Cilicia. Their schools furnished every region with male and female teachers, priests, vartabeds,[8] and so on. At the people's expense, they sent three capable

---

[7] [MA, TMB] The presence of Armenians in Aintab dates back to the Armenian Kingdom of Cilicia. Armenians of Aintab had been active in the sociocultural and economical life until the Hamidian massacres in 1895 and the Armenian Genocide in 1915.
[8] [MA, TMB] In the Armenian Apostolic Church the title is bestowed upon priests who have taken a vow of celibacy.

students to America or Europe every year and likewise funded the study of numerous pupils at the local American college, whose entire student body was Armenian.

Aintab was further flourishing economically: all kinds of fruits grew abundantly in the surrounding orchards, especially grapes and pistachios, which secured a large revenue for the city. Pistachios alone brought in 500,000 liras per year. After the reestablishment of the Ottoman Constitution, commerce increased, and Aintab became the economic center for the southwestern Armenian provinces (Sepasdia, Kharpert, Yerznga, Malatia,[9] etc.). Handcrafts were abundant and were controlled by the Armenians, especially the trade in woven goods, whose final products were distributed all over the country. Women's needlework was very valuable, especially in America. Two hundred thousand ghurush[10] worth of goods were bought weekly in the city of Aintab alone.

Being a mountainous city, Aintab's air is very clean; it has abundant and clear water and warm mineral springs. The people are well-formed, generally handsome, and bear very happy dispositions. During times of peace, this region almost always has a festive and cheerful appearance. Agriculture and viticulture have advanced considerably in the surrounding villages.

When the order for deportation came, some of the city's most wealthy succeeded one way or another in escaping through bribery. The government gave the population five days, after which time they began emptying the city, district by district. The people of Aintab hastily sold their homes and belongings. Either by cart, horse, camel, or donkey, they set out with relative comfort, abandoning their beautiful and prosperous city. The deportees were split into four or five branches. One group reached the Sajur station,[11] where they remained for a time, although living there was quite difficult.

A strange encounter took place when I was at Sajur. The Armenian soldiers from Aintab were being transferred with the Turkish army from Istanbul to Baghdad. When the train stopped and the soldiers deboarded for a moment to have some water, the Armenian soldiers suddenly noticed the great multitude of miserable and tearful deportees, who were huddled together in dispersed groups, in horror, awaiting their new orders. The soldiers recognize their fellow citizens and, no longer heeding any orders, approached them. They kiss and embrace;

---

[9] [MA, TMB] Armenian versions of place names are kept as in the original. They respectively correspond to Sivas, Harput (in Elazığ), Erzincan, and Malatya, in modern-day Turkey.
[10] [AM] Armenian transliteration of the Ottoman silver coin, or kuruş.
[11] [MA, TMB] Sajur, or today's Akcakoyunlu train station in Antep, Turkey.

children find their fathers; trembling old women clasp their sons in their arms; a clamor of crying and wailing dominates the air. The Armenian soldiers do not understand, cannot understand the reason behind this unexpected misfortune, and they turn to their colonel in protest.

What? They go to sacrifice their lives, and their families, their kids are subjected to this horrible position? What is the reason? What wrongs could these women and children have committed, while their husbands and fathers are serving in the Turkish army?

The colonel is also confused. He does not understand and strives to soften the rage of his Armenian soldiers, with whom he had no reason to be discontent until then. He reassures them and promises to make some sort of arrangement, when a strict order is suddenly delivered to the colonel, informing him that he is to conduct himself without restraint.

The strict orders come from all sides, separating the soldiers from the people, but the most brutal and severe means resolved nothing for the moment. Confusion and tumult reign as the clamor of people crying and the crack of the whip mix together. It is only with great effort and force that they barely succeed in pulling the Armenian soldiers from Aintab away from their defenseless families. They then lock the soldiers into the railway cars out of caution. The poor Armenians are thus separated, but the cries of rage, protest, and entreaty are still heard on both sides when the train hastily departs. Halfway along the road, as soon as they are able to, the Armenian soldiers throw themselves out the train's windows, trying to come to the aid of their families. They are pursued as rebels and deserters, and most are killed.

Meanwhile, the deported people of Aintab waiting at Sajur station were forced onto the road once more and sent to Bubuj (between the Euphrates and Aleppo).

The second group from Aintab was brought to Birecik, where they remained for twenty days to prepare rafts. The government had at first promised to help them with transportation. However, at the last minute, they told them that there was not enough wood, and so the people would have to travel on foot. At that point, the poor desperate Armenians collect the women's fine jewelry and hand them over to the government in exchange for the government to furnish them with the materials they would need to make their own rafts. That is why about 300 Armenians waited without shelter, while 15 pairs of rafts were being built. Every day, Turks and Kurds would approach the group and try to buy women and children, even though the Armenians rejected these propositions, in horror. Although the gendarmes overseeing the Armenians did not object, they fortunately did not allow the Turks and Kurds to behave brutally toward the Armenians when these propositions were rejected.

When the rafts had been built, the people set out on the Euphrates and arrived before Jarābulus. The overseeing gendarmes and the boatmen immediately visited the local kaymakam and asked his permission to throw the Armenians into the river. The kaymakam refused to give that order and explained that the Armenians had to reach their allotted destination.

Nevertheless, the people had given themselves over to extreme despair. They did not know where they were going, nor for what reason. They were a disorderly mass of men, women, and children—a mass that you would think had become devoid of all human feeling: the mother inattentive to her baby's cries; the people uncompassionate toward one another; and nobody even speaking to one another. One thought governed them all, one single question in their minds: What are they going to do to us? Some still believed that this was all temporary, an issue of one or two months, and that they would soon return to their birthplaces, but the majority were imbued with a frightful astonishment. An intense anxiety had dulled even their most natural feelings.

Thirty individuals from this group returned to Jarābulus on November 12, 1915. They were on their way to stand trial in Birecik. A pair of rafts had been broken up during their journey, and the Armenians had gone to an Arab village to repair them. The Turkish gendarmes denounced these Armenians as rebels and were returning them on foot through that long road to Birecik. Young and old alike, they arrived covered in dust, barefoot, and dressed in rags. They were worn out from exhaustion and misery. They had not been allowed to stop at any village to rest or regain their strength. They had been called deserting *khāyins*[12] and had become the playthings of the gendarmes' unscrupulousness. There were children among them, dragging from their mothers' skirts. Even their mother's hearts had grown cold, as the hopeless mothers answered their children's cries with their own sighs of pain. Young or sick, it made no difference to the executioners. They used the whip to force these unfortunate souls to advance at their horses' paces. And everywhere, the Turkish people greeted them with mockery and insult.

The other two groups from Aintab were sent by train to Hama and Homs, which are stops on the way to Damascus. In Jarābulus, there was an Armenian railway employee whose family was among these deportees. He received a letter

---

[12] [MA, TMB] *khāyin* is an Arabic word that can mean "traitor," "disloyal," and "unfaithful" among other things. What is interesting in the original is that Zabel Yesayan has used the word and then applied the Armenian plural marker *-ներ: խայիններ* (khāyinner).

in Turkish from his relatives, who said they were comfortable and that they were working in minor trades. In their places of exile, the rich and well-trained people of Aintab procured their daily living by occupying themselves as platers, coppersmiths, and weavers.

The deportation of the various regions of Cilicia took place successively. The Armenians of Marash and its vicinity, as well as Adana, Mersin, and Sis,[13] were similarly stripped of their homes, their wealth, their overall lives, which they had acquired through hard work and diligence. The wealthy remained in Aleppo and its environs. However, those who had no means of living outside their birthplaces became a burden to the government and were sent to Mesopotamia.

The deportation of Cilicia was organized by the commander of the Syrian army, Jemal Pasha, and its execution was overseen by Fakhri Pasha. The deportation of the inhabitants of Cilicia took place, comparatively, in an orderly manner—at least the men were not completely annihilated. After reaching their place of exile, the men were allowed to reunite with their families and, in a way, drag themselves through the difficult lives allotted to them.

---

[13] [MA, TMB] Mersin and Sis (now Kozan) were sanjaks (districts) of the Adana vilayet (province) in the Ottoman administrative system.

4

The Story of a Wealthy Village. The Sight of the Arriving Refugees. The Collapsed Woman. Nighttime Assaults. A Complaint to the Turkish Authorities.

There was a wealthy 150-home Armenian village north of Aintab, near the Euphrates. This village exported pistachios, from which it received a yearly gross income of 200,000 liras. When the deportation order becomes announced, the villagers are given two days to prepare for their departure. The surrounding Kurdish villagers had long envied the Armenians' position there. They often entered the village secretly and damaged the trees there. These trees constituted the source of those Armenians' wealth. And so, now, a very favorable opportunity arises to satiate their malice. The people condemned to deportation were still in the village when the Kurdish assault began; they ravaged and plundered, taking the Armenians' possessions to their own villages. At the same time, led by the Kurds, the gendarmes and soldiers were digging into the ground and demolishing walls in search of hidden gold. No one pitied the Armenians. Not a single friend was found even among the neighboring Muslim villagers, although the Armenians had sold their goods at very low prices (a hundred goats for two liras) and had given their cattle to the neighboring Kurds for nothing, telling them: *If we return alive, you'll give them back to us, but in the opposite case, they'll be yours (ḥalāl¹)*.

An Armenian villager, who witnesses this search and plunder, hopelessly takes to the road with the firm conviction that he is on the journey to his own death.

---

[1] [MA, TMB] *ḥalāl* is an Arabic word that translates to "permissible," indicating what is lawful and legitimate according to the Islamic law. In the Qur'an, the term *ḥalāl* is contrasted with the term *ḥarām*, meaning "forbidden."

The sorrowful caravan of deportees advances under the watch of ten gendarmes, who torment the Armenians according to their cruel whims. They divide the men and women into separate groups and do not even allow families to come together and help each other whenever the caravan stops at night. At the same time, the gendarmes subject groups of men to backbreaking labor. Having them smooth roads and clear stones, in addition to other similar tasks, the gendarmes do not allow the men a moment of rest. And sometimes, under different types of pretexts, the gendarmes would take the men to the bank of the Euphrates, only to suddenly throw them into the river, one-by-one. Whenever the women discovered that another group of men had disappeared, they became bitterly hopeless. Thinking their relatives might be among the dead, each one of them wailed—searching through tearful eyes for a son, a brother, or husband in the depths of a crowd, lost in the dust. If at any point during their journey, they encountered another group [of Armenians], upon chance, they were forbidden from speaking [to one another]; terrified, it was only their hopeless gazes alone that would meet one another. By the time the caravan reached Jarābulus, fifteen young men had been sent to their deaths in the river.

Every evening, once darkness had enveloped the world, the deportees would dismount from their donkeys and stop at the place chosen by their gendarmes. The women and children were alone and defenseless. Every night, they were attacked by not only the gendarmes assigned to watch them but also other gendarmes from surrounding areas. They stole whatever the Armenians had, such as finery and money, always leaving with a valuable booty.

It was toward the end of June that we heard in Jarābulus that Armenian emigrants would soon be arriving. We immediately saw the exiles descending the nearby hill. Fatigue and heat had changed them. The donkeys went in pairs; and on each one was a woman with a child in front of her and behind her. There was sometimes even one on her lap. The women had wrapped white linens around their heads to protect themselves from the sun. The journey's difficulties, along with their spiritual and physical suffering, had reduced them to such a terrible state, that it was impossible to distinguish the young from the elderly. The men presented a similar picture: sunburnt, parched, confused; it was as if they looked without seeing, and their movements had become disjointed under the influence of horror and pain.

And this is how they progressed, hurrying and obeying the gendarmes' brutal and hasty orders, when they came upon a stream that needed to be crossed. They dismounted like lunatics from their donkeys toward the stream, the water of which was dirty and murky. Man and animal, big and small, ran insatiably toward the water. In their haste, they had the aimless movements of people who had gone mad, wetting their legs and breasts without being able to bring their mouths to the water. Some collapsed, while many of the women—having lost all sense of indecency—hastily and angrily threw their clothes aside and entered naked into the water. This all took place in a strange silence and with strange speed. Some of the people's lips had hardly reached the water, when the gendarmes began yelling and threatening them. We heard these words amid the clamor of orders: *That's enough already, you've rested too much!* The thirsty Armenians were thrown into disarray as they reassembled without having satisfied their thirst. They looked for their donkeys, looked for each other, while the orders confused them even more. Trampling over one another, they wandered about as if they were possessed: as some gendarmes yelled and others threw blows. The children were dispersed here and there. The Kurds from the surrounding area, taking advantage of this confusion, would approach the children, turning their heads to see their faces. They wanted to hide the pretty ones under their *meshlah*s (overcoats), so they could take them away with them. I approached these Kurds, and I intervened, preventing them from kidnapping the children. The Armenians in Jarābulus still maintained their rights as citizens, and so my intervention was not fruitless.

The caravan of deportees was reassembled and slowly drew back to the road. An old woman remained on the bank of the river, her almost seventeen-year-old daughter falling over her, crying, and calling out to her mother. The woman had almost stopped breathing. Another elderly woman, the sister of the woman who had fainted, cried and sang an elegy (*meni*)[2] while beating her breast. Two old men used their *fezzes*[3] to transport water from the nearby stream, since they had no other vessel. They poured the water onto the collapsed woman, completely soaking the poor woman. Fortunately, the gendarmes were busy with the caravan and did not look back. Lost in their confusion and cries, the deportees progressed, raising a cloud of dust behind them. At the stream, the woman's sobs through her elegy were left to echo alone. Finally, a gendarme noticed the men carrying the water and called them over. They were forced to leave, and only the women remained, singing their cries. At that moment, a few Kurds, standing

---

[2] [ZY] The people from those areas have the custom of expressing their pain through song. [MA, TMB] An Armenian transliteration of mani in Turkish, meaning "folk songs" or "poems," sung or recited in Turkish.
[3] [MA, TMB] A short hat, made of felt, in the shape of a cylinder and with a tassel. It was commonly worn by men in the Ottoman Empire. The term comes from the city of Fez in Morocco, where most of the hats were once made.

silently and cruelly around them, waited for the caravan to disappear so they could ravish a young and beautiful girl.

I also stood there. Sensing the Kurds' intent, I would not leave. Finally, I considered it better to lead the girl and her aunt to the caravan, where those from their village were. I incited them to follow me. We claimed the mother dead, and covering her with a cloth, departed from the stream. We walked hastily, but the Kurds followed us for a long time and only disappeared once we approached the caravan. The elderly woman continued singing her sad song and sometimes turning toward her sister's corpse. Her daughter sobbed, her face lost behind her tears. Her knees were giving out, and she walked with difficulty.

The caravan arrived in Jarābulus and stopped before the *kaymakam*'s door to receive instructions. It was then that I noticed the group was comprised of 800 people. They had dismounted from their donkeys. Tired, hungry, wounded, spent, and broken, they awaited their orders with tears falling down their faces; their eyes were fixed on the windows of the governor's office. For an hour and a half, the deportees waited anxiously to receive their sentence. The *kaymakam* finally deigned to order that they immediately depart for the fields of a nearby village to spend the night. The gendarmes who oversaw the caravan demanded the 250 donkeys of the deportees as payment. Then, they gifted the five most beautiful white donkeys to the *kaymakam*. Afterward, I saw the *kaymakam*'s sons mount and ride those donkeys every day.

When I came back, I wanted to go and check on that woman we had claimed dead. But considering that the Kurds were tense against me, I did not go myself. Instead, I sent the local railroad night watchman, an Armenian-speaking Kurd named Ali *Dayi*.[4] In the dark, he approached her area and noticed a Kurd trying to rape that seventy-year-old, lifeless woman. Ali Dayi rushes upon the Kurd, who flees, taking the cover we had placed over the old woman with him. The woman was finally revived because the night was cool and because of Ali Dayi's efforts. He brought her to us late at night, and with his help and that of another Kurd, we sent her to the place where the exiles had stopped, so that she could rejoin her daughter.

Having heard that these villagers were wealthy, the commander of the local gendarmes hoped that they might still have gold and finery hidden on their persons. The commander attacks the group in the middle of the night with a few of his men. Since the poor villagers are woken suddenly, they become confused. Taking advantage of the tumult and confusion, the government officials begin

---

[4] [MA, TMB] dayı means maternal uncle in Turkish, though it is also used as a sign of respect.

searching the Armenians, one-by-one. They strip the men, women, and children, and plunder them, collecting their very last means: their money, gold, and finery. These unfortunate deportees from that wealthy village had not yet succeeded in hiding these things in the folds of their clothes.

It was the same night. Another group of Armenians, both men and women who had been deported from the villages on the right bank of the Euphrates, were spending the night in the open field near Jarābulus.

It was extremely dark that night; there was not a star in the sky; and the ground covered by black sand, flat, silent, and desolate. Even the Euphrates had turned black: its whitish current unnoticeable in that expansive darkness. The dogs stopped howling; there was not even a single whisper in that heavy and dark night.

The group of deportees had their own guards, who stood watch in turns—so that an assault would at least not take them by surprise. Since it was past midnight, the guards rise from their posts. There was a priest among them, and when he prayed the last prayer of the night, final prayer, every murmur stopped. The exhausted group buried themselves in a deep sleep.

The guarding gendarmes had intentionally moved away prior—and this fragmented group of people found themselves, in that moment, helpless and defenseless, on an unknown terrain of unfamiliar land.

The local railroad guard, a Circassian[5] named Mustafa Bey, and a Turkish officer named Hasan Effendi (who had been condemned to the gallows for having played a role in the Adana massacre but was later released), together with a few soldiers and a group of Circassians, searched in the dark with a single lantern for the Armenian deportees. The Circassians searched every corner, and finally, the heavy breathing of hundreds of unfortunate [Armenians] reached their sharpened ears. They approach [the area], find the group [of Armenians]; and fixing their bayonets, they crawl and disappear into the crowd. A few broken cries rise from here and there, and the group of exiles becomes agitated, in terror. The Armenians were still not entirely awake. The Circassians take advantage of the confusion of these initial moments to carry away six to seven girls. The Circassians tie the girls up and cover their mouths, then hasten back to plunder the rest of the Armenians.

---

[5] [MA, TMB] Circassians, also known as Cherkess or Adyghe, are an ethnic group that are indigenous to the historic region of Circassia in the Northwest Caucasus. After the genocide perpetrated on the Circassians by the Russian Empire in the nineteenth century, Circassians were exiled to Anatolia, eventually settling there and across the SWANA regions where most of them remain today.

At this point, many of the Armenians are awake, calling out to one another. And what cries they were! Perhaps, it was a bad dream that was disturbing them! How many times had they been awoken like this by nightmarish screams: when one or another of them has yelled in horror and dread under the influence of a bad dream! They are exhausted, and their weakened limbs are stuck in the damp sand. And because of their troubled souls, they do not want to move; and they whisper to one another: *There's nothing, there's nothing . . .*

Nonetheless, the elderly notice the light from a lantern and wake all the men. Coming together, they question anxiously: *What is that light?*

At that point, the Circassians and the soldiers assault the Armenians with the butts of their rifles and beat them with their feet. Some of the Armenians try to collect their families and pull them aside. Bewildered, many remain motionless: Are they asleep or awake? Which side are they attacking from? What do they want from them? A nightmarish confusion reigns. The darkness is so intense that they cannot distinguish between friend and foe. The assailants' spiteful panting, their curses, and maledictions are drowned out by the Armenians' collective cry of horror and pain, which can be heard everywhere and echoes unlike any human sound. In the confusion and darkness, bayonets meet one another, thrusting into warm bodies that palpitate with life and pain. The wounded and the children are trampled upon; and with aimless movements, the women run; they run and crash into one another; they strike one another—before falling, they call out the names of their loved ones with a sharp, final cry. *Mother . . . Hayganush . . . yavrum*[6] . . .

Near a lantern, a group of Circassians and soldiers calmly completes its organized intention. They search the exiles, one-by-one, stripping them, and taking whatever they can find; they fill their bags with money and finery. They also take their nice clothes; giving the owners of them rags in return, they move on to the next person. The women and girls do not want to strip in front of those brutes, but the Circassians rip their clothes off; the commander and his soldiers laugh and delight in the face of that pitiable sight.

Once they had finished plundering the Armenians, the Circassians and the soldiers departed. At that point, the gendarmes charged with overseeing the deportees come forward and order the Armenians to gather around the lantern. The scattered deportees begin to assemble themselves in the darkness. Fumbling in the dark, they collect the corpses of the children, untie the girls who had been raped, and began sobbing and lamenting.

---

[6] [MA, TMB] *yavrum* is a Turkish word meaning "my dear," "my darling," or "my little one."

Once we had been informed in detail about these events—and considering that the local *kaymakam* had shown a trace of goodness on other occasions—we took two young men from that same group and submitted a protest to the government. After listening to us, the *kaymakam* sent us to his assistant, who turned out to be Hasan Effendi, the same commander who had participated in the plunder.

Outraged by this audacity on the part of Armenians, Hasan Effendi made some insulting remarks and sent us to Mustafa Bey, a Circassian. When the two young deportees saw the Circassian, they turned pale and told me that this man had led the brigands on the previous night. The Circassian had known me for a long time. He turned his harsh eyes to me and angrily and menacingly said: *You led them, didn't you? You incited these khāyins to protest. Just wait, the time will come. It will not be like this forever.*

Then, turning to the young men, he said severely: *Come! Let's go find these villains.*

He had taken them to the old fortress on the bank of the Euphrates, and after whipping them for a long time with his leather lash, he stabbed them both and threw their corpses onto the riverbank.

This incident would become the reason for my departure from Jarābulus several months later. The local Armenian workers protested to the German railroad company. Mustafa Bey was removed from his post, and Hasan Effendi was greatly bothered. The complaint even reached Jemal Pasha.

And the group of exiles, who were supposed to stay and rest near Jarābulus for a few days, were made to leave that very same day for Mesopotamia.

5

An Armenian Mother. Children Are Sold Off. The Role of a Greek Woman.

Rachel wept for her children,
and she did not want to be comforted, since they were no more.[1]

In the month of July, a group of Armenians from the vicinity of Birecik, and various other places along the bank of the Euphrates, arrived at the Jarabulus station. The group was made up of 1,620 people altogether: both men and women, along with their priests. They were going to depart by train the following day. The uneven, rocky field next to the station was set aside for them to spend the night. Part of the exiles had traveled on foot and another part by donkey, but their donkeys were confiscated in Jarabulus. The local officials told the deportees that they would no longer need their animals, since they would be continuing by train.

In the evening, the Armenians began preparing their places to sleep. They were collecting the rocks and evening out the soil, when they suddenly stopped, noticing that the ground underneath the stones was muddy. It had rained heavily two days before, and the water had remained in pools beneath the rocks. The intense daytime heat had been followed by a piercing cold, and the damp ground made the situation unbearable. They were so tired and in such pain from the torturous journey that the deportees began spreading out over the field. They were not allowed to go beyond a certain point, and so, they sat on the rocks, spread out their weary limbs; and many of them, exhausted, threw themselves onto the damp sand. Only the children rested in their mothers' laps. However, the ones who were a bit older, unable to endure the torments they had borne on the road, cried and wailed. Hearing these stirring cries of supplication, we

---

[1] [MA, TMB] Rendered by Zabel Yesayan in the Classic Armenian: Հռաքէլ լայր զորդիս իւր և ոչ կամէր մխիթարիլ, զի ոչ էին (Mt. 2:18). Our translation.

went to see what was happening. When we learned of the unbearable state that these thousands of people has been put in, we strongly urged the priests to take a handful of people and come before the *kaymakam,* asking him permission to sleep in the vast empty storehouses next to the station. The *kaymakam bey*—who had seen that horrible sight and whose ears had heard the ill-fated population's supplications and lamentations—refused to admit the supplicants, and instead began yelling from his bed without opening the door: *No! No! I don't want to. Olmaz, olmaz...*[2].

Hopeless, the deportees spent the night on that damp soil. I saw them when the morning came. To protect themselves from the cold, they had instinctively come together, were pressed against one another, joined together; they made up one large, lifeless, almost uniform, mass. They had become silent and stupefied, and they were so petrified in their positions that you would think they could never again be separated.

The sun had risen considerably by the time the *kaymakam bey* went out with his wife and children. They were joined by the railway inspector, a Greek by the name of Koynopulos Effendi, and his wife. Dressed in ornamented silk, the women advances forward: haughty, happy, smiling and laughing, as if she were going to a wedding. This group was coming toward the exiled Armenian. When the priest saw that the *bey* was approaching them, he ran over to meet him. He put his hands on the breast of his torn cassock. Then, he bowed to the ground, and with quivering lips, mumbled his greeting and best wishes.

The *bey* expressed his desire to walk among the deportees. The miserable priest, confused and distressed, hastened to his flock [of Armenians] and began yelling hoarsely:

> Get up! Stand up, the kaymakam bey is coming to see you. Meet him with a satisfied look. Don't cry! Don't beg! Stand and greet him. The kaymakam bey is coming to see you.

The people were agitated and fearful, trembling in anticipation; they later gathered themselves and waited.

Continuing their discussion and laughter, the Turks and Greeks approached the Armenians. A painful, then a forced smile appeared on the priest's anxious face, as he turned to the guests. He cast a horrified gaze at a few of the deportees, alerting them that they are not standing with the necessary respect—they were bent over in pain and suffering.

---

[2] [MA, TMB] Turkish expression meaning "it is not possible," or "it is not likely."

The *kaymakam* walks among the groups, observing the children; he begins examining and questioning them. The deportees understand that the *bey* is looking for a child. A shudder of fear passes over all the mothers, as each one of them tries to hide her child underneath her skirt. Hands shake with anxiety; gazes wander; and one woman, having lost her mind, cries:

> Oh Lord, God of our fathers, for which of our sins is this hour an atonement?

The *bey* frowns and stops. His walk was proven to be fruitless: he had not found what he desired. The children's resistance, their fleeing, their thin and ugly appearance—all of it had him discouraged.

Noticing the *bey*'s bad disposition, the trembling priest bows once more. He greets the bey and attempts to smile with his face grimaced with horror, swallowing his tears. But the *bey* is enraged. And despite the priest's humble conduct, despite the miserable Armenians' reverential greeting, the *bey* grabs the priest from his breast and, shaking him, screams:

> Where are the good children? Where have you kept them, you khāyin? I want them! I want the pretty children now!

A shower of curses and threats rained down on the population and the elderly priest, who, now baffled, nearly gone mad, the priest turns to his flock and attempts to imitate the *kaymakam*'s anger:

> Janem,[3] hand them over, bring your children forward. Hand them over, hand everything over. Don't anger the kaymakam bey.

The entire group thunders with rage and malediction. In the depths of their desperation, they forget their fear, their instinctual caution, which had kept them silent. Confused, the priest turns to the *kaymakam*, who is still yelling, then turns to his flock, whose rage gradually fades into a plaintive moan. Old women mumble hopeless prayers, and no one dares to move. It is as if they are all waiting for a catastrophe, unseen.

At that moment, the wife of the Greek inspector, seeing the *kaymakam*'s anger, approaches him and tries to calm him down with tender words.

> Don't be angry, my bey, she says, obsequiously. I'll get the pretty kids out. You don't know how cunning these Armenians are. I'll find them, you just relax.

And Koynopulos Effendi similarly tries to calm the bey and says:

---

[3] [MA, TMB] *canım* is a Turkish word of endearment, meaning "my dear." Here it is used as a filler meaning "well."

Wait just one minute, bey, my wife will presently bring you what you desire.

Mrs. Koynopulos slides herself among the groups of Armenians, where she is received by harsh, silent, and tear-soaked faces. It is as if even the youngest children sense that they are the ones in danger, as they instinctively stand quiet. Not a single child cries in that heavy and severe moment.

The Greek woman finally finds a nine-year-old orphan girl, whose father had died as a soldier in the Turkish army, and whose mother died on the road during the deportations. She was a pretty girl with a thin face; she had light skin, black eyes, and abundant hair. She covered her head with a black *yazma*,[4] which had been her mother's mourning *yazma*. She was sad and heart broken. However, her pretty face was pleasing to the bey's *hanem*,[5] and since she had no one to protect or watch over her, she was sent with a soldier to the bey's home.

Before leaving, she looked at the group of Armenian deportees, her head bent, and she seemed to hesitate to approach them. Her sorrowful eyes were saying:

Will no one give me one last kiss?

Her neighbor's wife guessed the orphan's thoughts. She called her over and said:

Come, I will kiss you in place of your mother.

And having kissed her on both cheeks, she handed the girl over to the enemy.

The *kaymakam bey* had calmed down somewhat, and the Greek woman, emboldened, entered once more into the group and this time looked for a young boy, because the *kaymakam* preferred to buy a boy. Lively and hasty, the Greek woman looked everywhere, as the Armenian mothers bent their eyes to the ground, not wanting their gazes to meet the Greek woman's eyes. She finally pulled a pretty boy out from under the skirts of one of the deportees. The mother cried, begged, and kissed the Greek woman's hands and feet. But Mrs. Koynopoulous was barren, and nature had deprived her of motherly feelings. Paying no attention to the mother's tears, she began screaming:

Bey, bey, come here! Look how pretty he is!

The *bey* approached them and smiled: this little boy was to his taste. He was hardly six years old, chubby, with light skin, and dark eyes. The Greek woman endeavored to pull the boy away from his mother, who in turn made a superhuman effort to protect her child, holding him tightly to her chest. Taking

---

[4] [AM] A headscarf.
[5] [AM] In this case, the *bey*'s wife.

his mother's desperate embrace for a caress, the little boy raised his head, kissed his mother's face, and showed her the nickel piece the *bey* had given him.

The Greek official had joined his wife; and in front of the bey, the two of them together evaluated the boy, praising how beautiful, healthy, and good he was. Terrified by what she saw, the poor mother wanted to flee with her child and disappear into the crowd, but the *kaymakam* ordered his soldiers to hold her and block her escape.

Seeing the mother's resistance, which gradually rises to fury, the *bey* curses the gendarmes, slams his foot onto the ground, and shakes his head in rage. Throwing all his anger at the priest, he yells:

> The boy must immediately be handed over to the soldiers, so they can take him home.

The boy's father was standing to the side, looking at all this, dumbfounded, as if he had lost all human emotion. The priest approached him and said:

> If your child doesn't go with them. . . . Have you thought about what will befall us? The kaymakam bey is furious. . . . Have you thought about what will happen to all these people?

The priest made the sign of the cross, as if to avert a clear and heavy threat.

The father mechanically approached his wife. Fear and fatherly love made him tremble, but he extended his arms and carried the boy, whose mother entrusted him to his father as a stronger and more trustworthy protector.

The father handed the child over to the soldiers. When the mother saw that her husband's bosom was empty, she understood. She pulled at her hair, clawed at her face, and, coming upon her husband, yelled ceaselessly:

> Who did you give my child to? Bring my boy back to me!

The *bey*'s group had completed their tour, and having paid the priest one *mejid*[6] for the boy, they departed. Since the orphan girl had no guardian, they paid nothing for her. The Greek woman, with the *kaymakam*'s permission, chose a fifteen-year-old girl to be her servant.

The *bey* ordered that the deportees be loaded into railway cars and hastily sent away. The exiled ones piled into the cars in rows. The woman who lost her child had not moved at all. She cried, wailed, said *menis*.[7] Having collected stones into a grave-like pile, she hit her head against the ground and cried with

---

[6] [MA, TMB] Ottoman coin worth twenty kuruş.
[7] [MA, TMB] Armenian transliteration of Turkish word, *mani* meaning "folk songs" or "poems."

an inconsolable sorrow. Her face had become distorted by the abundance of her tears. It was as if she had lost all human appearance. Each one of those exiled people was burdened by so much personal suffering that, inattentive to the mother's pain, they passed her and left. Her husband stood at the edge of the field, hopeless, forsaken, his eyes downcast. He did not dare to approach his wife.

But the inconsolable mother's weeping and lamentations reached the *kaymakam*, and these hopeless cries made him uncomfortable. He ordered the soldiers to take her away by force, to muffle out that sound. The gendarmes wanted to take her away, to lock her in one of the railway cars, but the mother fought back. She beseeched and implored them not to take her and to return her child to her. The woman's tears had almost entirely flooded the gendarmes' boots, but they needed to carry out the *bey's* order. They began dragging her off without heeding her supplications. Her clothes tore and her legs and feet bled as they dragged her over the rocks. This is how they delivered that woman to the train, throwing her nearly lifeless body into one of the cars.

In the *bey's* home, the children were given clothes and sweets. Every effort was made to win them over. The boy was dressed in colorful clothing, but the girl refused to change:

> I don't want red clothes: I need to wear black, she insisted.
> How come, my girl? they said, caressing her.
> My father and mother are dead—I am in mourning.

One month had passed, and the nine-year-old orphan still covered her head with her black *yazma*. All their efforts were in vain. Never, not once, did a smile appear on her indignant and sorrowful face. Sad and mournful, she remained apart from the others, isolated in her unconquerable grief. Affected by her stubborn sadness, and fearing that the mourning girl would bring misfortune onto their home, they renounced her and sent her on the road to Mesopotamia with another group of Armenian deportees.

6

The Distribution of Bread. The First Corpses on the Euphrates. Seventy Children Drowned.

In the same month, a 200-person group of Armenians arrived from the environs of Rumkale[1] in Cilicia and stopped near Jarabulus. They were supposed to leave the same day, but since they had eaten nothing for one and a half days, it was decided that the distribution of bread would take place in Jarabulus. The *kaymakam* ordered bread to be hastily baked. The bread was taken out of the oven, still uncooked, half of it was dough. It was then handed to Ali Dayi and me to distribute among the deportees. We filled two bags with bread. Two deportees were brought to us. We loaded their sacks with bread and set off. They groaned under the weight of their loads. They were very hungry. That is why whenever Ali and I moved somewhat ahead, they found the energy to steal and eat bread from their packs. When we arrived near the deportees, we immediately arranged for the priest and one of the notables to inform us of the number of members in each family, so that we could distribute the bread fairly. Ali Dayi and I were seated, each of us holding a bag, but the starving multitude came upon us. It became impossible to keep any sense of order. I began handing loaves to the women, but the men and the strong ones seized them from their hands. One would think these people were not men, but rather brutes maddened by hunger, all of whom had lost all traces of humanity. In the blink of an eye, they ate and devoured the bread. Leaving the bags, we barely managed to escape. Pregnant women, children, and the sick were left hungry. At one moment, I saw gaunt children licking the tips of their fingers and collecting the very last morsels fallen on the ground.

We always knew what was happening in Cilicia, following the events there. But we had no word at all from Armenia. This is how we first encountered Armenians from Armenia:

---

[1] [MA, TMB] Rumkale also known as Urumgala, is a fortress on the Euphrates, located in the province of Antep (Anitab).

Early in the morning of May 1, some friends and I wanted to go down to the bank of the Euphrates. Our region is beautiful in that season: it is as if you are living in a flower-garden, and the scent of wildflowers undulate in waves of tepid air. As we approached the river, we saw black masses wavering on the waters of the Euphrates. Arabs and the Turkish soldiers stood in groups and watched the masses with interest. Suddenly, someone cried:

They're Armenians, Armenians!

I approached one of the groups and asked a Turkish soldier:

What are these?

Heh! khayins, he responded. They're the corpses of your Armenians. You have no idea what's happened up ahead [of the river].

We did not want to believe him. Approaching the riverbank, we hastened upstream toward the appearing masses.

In a hollow on the riverbank, we saw a soldier seated at the water's edge. He was taking the coat, clothes, and shoes off a corpse.

We again did not want to believe that those corpses were Armenian. We thought, perhaps, they were the bodies of soldiers fallen in the war. We gathered around the Turkish soldier, and wanting to ascertain the truth, we approached the corpse. The soldier was rummaging through the pockets of the looted coat when he pulled out a notebook. I immediately took it from his hands. The water had rendered the letters unreadable. I gathered only this much: this was the logbook of a grocer from the village of Samsat.[2]

Fear and dread walled us in: so, they really were Armenians. The corpses traveled downstream, in groups of five or ten people who were all tied at their hands and feet. It was rare to find individual bodies; these were similarly tied up.

We would watch the river during the day, while it was still light out, our eyes fixed on it. Until May 5, 150–200 corpses passed us daily, not counting the ones that passed us during the night. This lasted until May 28–29, the daily number gradually diminishing.

The heaps of corpses tied together flowed, passed ceaselessly. There were the corpses of women too; there were children tied between each of their legs and under each of their arms. The women were entirely naked and young; there were no old women.

---

[2] [ZY] On the bank of the Euphrates, northeast of Aleppo.

In that same hollow, I encountered the body of a girl who appeared to be fourteen years old. When I first saw her at a distance, she appeared only as a black mass. When she reached us, a wave threw her onto the riverbank, where she rested after turning for a moment in the current. At first, we saw only swelling: her stomach was black and grey. Her breasts were also swollen, and in such a way that they looked like they belonged to a woman. Her legs jutted out into the water, and her copper-colored thighs carried traces of wounds. Her ripped undergarments, which were soiled by dirt and blood, hung from her legs. Her hands were delicate and tied by a thick rope. Her face was lost in the water, but her abundant hair floated on the river's surface.

Another Armenian official and I had gone to the new bridge. There we saw the following: the guards stationed beneath the bridge had made long hooked iron poles, which they used to pull the corpses over to loot their clothing. When we came upon this, a soldier was pulling in a woman's corpse. He brought it over to the water's edge. The woman's body was white as chalk and carried massive black stains. Her body had transformed, had almost entirely festered; and the outline of her face had disappeared. Her body was so rotten that no sooner had the pole touched her than it thrust in effortlessly. The soldier took a silver ring from this corpse.

Beneath the same bridge, a surveyor's aide—a Frenchman there under the name of a Greek—approaches on his break to wash his hands in the Euphrates, when something suddenly clings to his arm. He pulls this up in terror. It was the corpse of a fourteen- or fifteen-year-old girl. The young man frees his hand from the girl's hair, but nearby Kurds approach him and loot her corpse. She was still young and beautiful. Her corpse was fresh and had not changed at all. A rock was tied to her foot, which made her move downstream slowly and then sunk underwater, without rising back to the surface.

We observed an unusual sight some distance from Jarābulus: flocks of crows and packs of dogs appeared, cawing, howling, and moaning of which could be heard for a long time during the twilight hours. Curious, we went to that area to see what was happening. While we were still on the road, we saw in the fields: pieces of human bodies, hands, half-broken skulls, and such. Who were these people? Where had they come from? We could not make it out. We saw massive dogs pull pieces off from the corpses and take them to their dens to feed their young. And by the riverbank, the human pieces were so plentiful that the packs of dogs and flocks of crows and various other wild birds sat perched on their prey, undisturbed, without hurting one other. They thrust their mouths and beaks into the bodies, devouring without a pause.

The Aleppo central bureau chief and rail line supplier of the German railroad was a Swiss. He left for the Karadagh[3] forest to procure wood. He was, however, unable to continue his journey along the Euphrates. The heaps of corpses on both sides of the river between Birecik and Karadagh gave off such a foul odor, and their appearance frayed his nerves so profoundly that he fled in horror and became fatally ill on his return to Aleppo.

When the Armenians from Adıyaman, Samsat, and the surrounding villages were deported, the women were sent to the Arap Pınar station. The men are tied together and thrown into the river. Toward the end of May, the women from those areas were being sent by train (forty cars, each of which were holding about sixty people) to Aleppo. As they cross the temporary bridge over the Euphrates, those unfortunate ones look out the windows of the cars and see a group of corpses on the river; their clothing and appearance look similar to that of their villagers. A newlywed, who had given birth to her first child in the train and, due to her wealth and beauty, had been subjected to unspeakable suffering on the road, had become half-mad. She thinks she recognizes her husband's corpse among this group. All the women scream and want to fall into the river: they cry out the names of their beloveds; they shout; they wail; and their voices rise so high that they drown out the train's incessant whistle.

In a maddened state, the newlywed wants to throw herself into the river. Failing to jump out from the narrow window, she throws her newborn child toward her supposed husband. Falling on the rocks, her baby immediately crashes there and dies.

A Turk—feigning that he will hand Armenian children over to the care of good people—gathers seventy children from a group of Armenians from Samsat and from a group collected by Turks. This Turk loads the children onto a raft and says that he will take them to Jarābulus over the Euphrates, and that they will move on, from there, to Aleppo.

When they arrive near *Supurgiji (Surp Prgich)*[4]—where there is a big waterfall that is extremely dangerous for any kind of boat—he breaks off one of the planks, jumps into the water, and swims over to the riverbank. Abandoned and without a rudder, the children's raft reaches the waterfall, capsizes immediately, and the terrified children become scattered and flow with the tide beneath the water.

---

[3] [MA, TMB] Arasbârân (lit. "banks of the Aras"), also known as Qaradagh, is a large mountainous area stretching from the Qūshā Dāgh massif to the Aras River. In the second century BC, the Armenian principality Parspatunik was established in this region, extending through the Armenian Genocide of 1915 until present day.

[4] [AM] *Supurgiji* is a local variation of *Surp Prgich*, which translates to "Holy Savior."

Not half an hour later, seventy tiny corpses are directed downstream. Standing on the riverbank, the Turks watch and wait until the last child disappears, then return to their village.

The Armenians in our region were subjected to unspeakable spiritual torments. When corpses appeared on the river, the local Armenians left their work, or whatever they were doing, and fled to avoid this sight. And the black masses of the drowned bodies kept passing by, without a pause. Rather than moving the Turks' pity, these masses provoked their hatred. Seated in their coffeehouses, Birecik's Turks hurled insults at the passing corpses or derided and mocked them. The boys threw stones and followed the bodies' movements with offensive remarks from the riverbank, while the women complained that those filthy corpses had dirtied the Euphrates, directing all kinds of maledictions and denigrations at the Armenians.

Only the Arabs had pity and complained. Their leaders were infuriated by these unjust and unscrupulous acts. The deaths of the seventy children, especially, provoked them against the Turks. They protested vehemently to the government in Aleppo. Having taken custody of the criminal who murdered the seventy children, they handed him over to the court. He was then hanged due to the insistence / influence of the Arabs.

In many places, I was thought to be a Muslim. And so, the Turks spoke to me about these events without restraint. Their general opinion was as follows:

> God created the Armenians for *kurban* (sacrifice)[5] and their women for pleasure, but murdering children is truly barbaric.

---

[5] [MA, TMB] *kurban* is a Turkish word meaning "victim." The word comes from the Arabic *qurbān* or *udhiyah* as referred to in Islamic law, meaning "sacrificial animal." The concept and definition of the word is derived from the Qur'an (same idea in the korban in Judaism and the κουρμπάνι [kourbania] in parts of Greece) where a ritual animal sacrifice is performed during the Eid al-Adha.

7

Episodes from the Deportations of Armenians from Armenia. Dikranagerd. Mardin. In Resulayn. In Tell Abyad. In Edessa.[1] Arap Pınar.

A few very wealthy bankers from Dikranagerd, by paying a substantial bribe, had left the city. But on the road, the men are separated from their families and murdered between Siverek and Edessa. Their wives and daughters, about 200 people, reach a safe place and recount the following incidents, which they had followed day by day:

At first, the government seizes 650 Armenians from Dikranagerd and its environs and sends them on rafts over the Tigris toward Mosul. But after gaining some distance from the city, the gendarmes tear apart the goatskin straps supporting the rafts, and the exiled ones fall into the river. Those who manage to swim to the riverbank are shot dead by the gendarmes waiting there.

After this incident, the Armenian men are taken away from Dikranagerd in groups. This is done in order of their position and wealth. They are buried alive in wheat silos, which are then covered over with stones. Another group is taken to the bank of the Tigris and drowned. The rest of them, both men and women, are sent in groups to Resulayn via Mardin. On the road, they separate the women from the men. Even boys as young as six are taken to valleys, where they are massacred. Before reaching Mardin, the women are assaulted by Chechens, who mercilessly rape the most beautiful girls, while the Kurds continue to plunder the women. While the men are being massacred, the women are made to stand off to the side. They hear the dying wails of the men in the valleys. The massacres of the Armenians from Dikranagerd and its surrounding villages were so violent that all the valleys from Dikranagerd to Mardin were filled with corpses, and from Siverek to Edessa, both sides of the road were covered in them. Only a

---

[1] [MA, TMB] now Urfa, Turkey.

pitiful group of broken, plundered, and dishonored women, who are old, reach Resulayn from Dikranagerd's prosperous Armenian-populated region.

A Turkish soldier who had been wounded in the fighting at Van, and who had reached Jarabulus by the same road, recounted the following:

> In Bitlis, I saw that Armenian merchants had been made to carry account books, and that they were being transported thus to Siirt. Armenian soldiers, who had been brought from Erzrum to work on the construction of a fort, return with merchants from Bitlis even before finishing their work. There, by Dzag kar,[2] both the soldiers and the merchants are assaulted by the local Kurds, who plunder and kill them.

On the Bitlis-Siirt road, in an Armenian village, I saw an Armenian woman hanging from her feet. Her head hung 1 meter off the ground. Her three children's feet were nailed to the ground, as well. The children were still alive, and they stretched out to reach one another. Turkish soldiers were standing at a distance and used the woman's swinging body as target practice, sending bullets toward her eyes and breasts.

The woman's crime was that she had hidden with her children to escape the deportation.

Mardin—Immediately after the deportations from Dikranagerd, the deportation and massacre of Mardin began, under the supervision of Memduh Bey. Men are gathered on the grounds that they will be put to work, to renovate the roads. As soon as the authorities take the Armenian men out of the city, they massacre them in the valleys of Dikranagerd and Mardin.

In Baghdad, a Turkish soldier told me that all the valleys were filled with corpses, and that those piles reached nearly half the valleys' depths. The blood of the men who had been stabbed was so abundant that it flowed like water.

Mardin's women and girls were subjected to the same fate as those from Dikranagerd. The Chechens picked out the most beautiful ones, plundered the convoy, and sent the survivors to Resulayn. In this region, one group of Assyrians became subjected to the same fate as the Armenians. An Assyrian woman recounted the following, all the while cursing the Armenians, who had become the cause of their misfortune:

> In Mardin, the deportation order produced a state of horror, because scattered groups of women from Dikranagerd and its environs had been arriving in the city. Their appearance, especially their cries and lamentations, made it clear what

---

[2] [ZY] One of Bitlis's noteworthy places.

awaited the deportees. At the same time, before the population had even left, the gendarmes, Chechens, and Kurds entered into the homes of the Armenians, plundering, beating, and raping them. Many lost their minds, and crying and bellowing, they moved along the roads, which had turned into a grand bazaar. In every corner, furniture and had rugs fallen and were piled up; objects were smashed; mirrors, porcelain, and other fragile vessels were shattered underfoot; and amidst all of this, corpses had fallen here and there; rape was present before everyone's eyes. The daughters of notable and decent families were subjected to the most extreme kinds of dishonor. The youngest and most beautiful, having been collected in various places, were sold to Muslims who had come from the surrounding area. About three hundred daughters of wealthy families from Dikranagerd and Mardin, who were the heiresses to great fortunes, were sold by Chechens, each for two hundred to three hundred liras.

The deportations of Dikranagerd, Mardin, Siirt, and Kharpert were organized by Halil Bey, who had come from Istanbul for this specific purpose. He had arranged çetes[3] [armed bands] made up of Arnavuts,[4] Chechens, and Circassians. Their purpose was to exterminate all of the Armenians. All this was kept secret, both from the Armenian and the Turkish populations, up until the date of the plan's execution. The deportation from these areas took place in the most barbaric manner: the men massacred, and the women and children subject to all kinds of torments.

In Resulayn—My friend, an employee with the railroad company, whose work took him regularly to Resulayn, recounted the following:

The first time I arrived in Resulayn, I saw thousands of people; women and children were crowded together over a wide space, on either side of the station and the railroad tracks. Chechens, Circassians, Turkish soldiers and officers would enter among those groups freely, returning every time with girls, property, finery, money, and such. I was informed that these were fragments of the deported populations of Dikranagerd and Mardin, including a smaller group from Kharpert. At first, the deportees were still rather well-dressed. However, as I commuted back and forth over the course of a week, the group grew little-by-little and these people's condition worsened. Misery, hunger, and spiritual and physical torments had changed them. Reduced to beggars, they would wander all over and pour onto the trains. Having so lost their instincts of self-preservation, they would carelessly fall beneath the wheels. The trains would return bloodied

---

[3] [AM] Çete in Turkish, which itself means "armed band" or "gang," were armed bands that participated in the killing of Armenians during the genocide.
[4] [AM] Albanian.

every time, having crushed another child. I secretly joined groups of exiled Armenians a few times and sensed their agony. Hungry, discolored, gaunt, and nearly reduced to corpses, they implored that I bring them bread. I would bring five sacks of flour with me every time and distribute the flour hastily. But, whenever the soldiers and gendarmes saw flour in these people's hands, they would take it by force to sell it to others. Being so close to death, hopelessness had taken a great hold over them. Women threw themselves beneath oncoming trains. Not only did the Turkish soldiers not offer any resistance to these suicides, but also standing nearby, they would watch and mock them. I even saw some Turkish soldiers line up women and a few children on the tracks and then roll a car down towards them. The soldiers laughed loudly as the Armenians were crushed, and as the injured writhed in pain.

Hunger, heat, and their overseers' pitiless behavior had established such an unbearable life for these exiles, that their cries of agony reached as far as Aleppo and brought forth an agitation among the non-Turkish population. To get ahead of their outrageous wrongdoings, the government decided to take the Armenians away, transferring them to Mdzpin (Nusaybin).

Wanting to save at least a few children before the Armenians' departure, my friend turned to the following means. He would have a few big baskets with him, which he used to transport turkeys from various places to Aleppo. He decided to use these baskets to help the Armenians. Collecting children from the fields every day, he would place them in the baskets and transport them to Aleppo. This is how he explained the impressions he bore while serving as these children's savior:

> I approached a group. They were all lying down, their faces in the ground to protect themselves from the sun. They were motionless and silent: you would think they were heaps next to each other in a cemetery, arranged in an unplanned and disorderly manner. I approached a child and wanted to wake him; but when I touched him, he did not budge. Thinking him asleep, I picked him up off the ground and saw that he was a good-looking boy. I immediately noticed that his eyes, half-open, were collapsing. The child was breathing his last breath. Shuddering, I left him on the ground and began running like a madman to escape that ill-omened sight. My soul was so profoundly disturbed that I lost all sense of reality. I remained there for hours, dumbfounded; my eyes were fixated without seeing. When I came back to myself, I saw a pregnant woman who, having left her two children behind, kissed my hands and beseeched me for a piece of bread.
>
> The sun had gone down considerably, and the scorching heat of midday had abated. I turned my eyes towards the group of children and saw that most of them had awoken and were stirring in place. I stood up and approached them again.

Women bewildered by hunger searched in the field for grass to eat, but everything had dried up over that sandy and scorched terrain. Meanwhile, the children, who looked like corpses, were so exhausted that they could only caress the pieces of dried grass, without the strength to pull them out of the hard ground.

I brought bread with me the next time. When I would show them the bread, so that they would come towards me, their eyes, which had lost their light up to that point, took on a feverish, almost mad lustre, fixating on me and the bread in my hand. They would try to get up and run towards me, but would fall on the hard ground and bloody their arms and faces. When I would approach a child to hand them a piece of bread, they would not take it; rather, they would ravish it, clawing at my hands. They had lost all childish grace and appearance: they had wrinkled faces, with rough gazes and animal-like expressions. They could not speak; yet when they wished to cry out, they would release a sort of panting and broken guttural clamor, which did not resemble a human syllable. Once, I approached a little one who had managed to maintain a sort of liveliness in his face, and I convinced him to come with me. He stared at me without responding, but I felt that he understood. It was then that I urged him to bring the other children with him, too. But he just pointed to the others, one-by-one, with a strange motion. I came closer and saw that they were all dead, that he was sitting there alone among corpses.

With his turkey baskets, that official brought forty to fifty children to Aleppo, and they were adopted by local Armenian families.

The Armenians from Resulayn were transferred to Mdzpin. Only the corpses remained, which they had made the surviving Armenians pile into a mound. The corpses remained like this, unburied; they decomposed and came to nothing under the scorching rays of the sun.

In Tell Abyad[5]—Khaled Bey, an Arab doctor with the railroad company, told me about the Armenians who had stopped in Tell Abyad. He was traveling by train, when he saw children fallen on the tracks. He makes the train stop. When he approached the children, he finds that, of the six there, only one is still alive. The rest are already dead. They move the tiny corpses off the tracks; and picking up the only living boy, Khaled Bey returns to the car. The boy was intelligent. After he becomes conscious, he explains how they had come to be there. Their group of deportees was traversing the region's mountains and valleys. Suddenly, the boy loses sight of his mother. He flees from the group to try and find her. After wandering for two days, he hears the train's whistle and goes in that

---

[5] [MA, TMB] A town in northern Syria. Armenian survivors of the Genocide became its first inhabitants.

direction. He finds the other children near the tracks; they were, like him, six or seven years old: lost, hungry, and abandoned.

> When you met them, were they all alive? the doctor asks.
>
> In the morning, we were still talking to each other, then one-by-one, they went quiet and fell, responds the child.

The Armenians in Tell Abyad were fragments of the deportees from Kharpert, Siverek, Chnkush,[6] and Chermug.[7] About 400 people were crowded into a small *khan*,[8] where there could hardly have been room for 50 or 60 people. They had no choice but to stand or sit on top of each other. Since the gendarmes forbade them from going outside to relieve themselves, they were nearly covered in feces and other filth. Their stench, their uncleanliness had fatal consequences; as the deportees were tormented by all manner of illnesses, many deaths occurred daily in that *khan*. The dead would lean onto the living. And since there was no room to fall, they would sometimes remain upright in the dense rows for a long time. The living were forced to either sit on the dead or take them in their arms, since it was impossible to move out of the way. Despite this extreme situation—despite their being hungry, half-dead, naked, and lost in filth and putrefaction—these Armenians had become playthings for the gendarmes, who would enter the *khan* at night and try to plunder them. The gendarmes would search the Armenians and demand their finery—but not finding anything, they would subject the population to all degrees of torture and dishonor.

From Tell Abyad to Arap Pınar, the railroad tracks were completely covered in the blood of Armenian women and children. On both sides of the line, one finds an endless string of corpses crushed by trains. This is because the Turkish gendarmes would have the Armenians they were meant to guard, sit on the tracks during the nighttime marches. These poor wretches from the depths of [Western] Armenia do not know what railroad tracks are; they had no idea about trains; and as they sleep stretched out on the tracks, extremely tired and spent, the oncoming train would surprise them. The train becomes forced to stop over corpses every time. One-by-one, the workers on the train would throw the crushed corpses off to the side and would make the survivors clear the tracks.

The Arab tribe of Anez,[9] having received large sums from the Armenians of Edessa, had come to Tell Abyad to save some of the Armenians. During the

---

[6] [MA, TMB] Now Çüngüş, a district in Diyarbakır.
[7] [MA, TMB] Now Çermik, a district in Diyarbakır.
[8] [MA, TMB] A type of inn commonly found in the Middle East that functioned as a trading center and hostel.
[9] [MA, TMB] The reference here is to the 'Anizah, an autonomous tribal group that predates the rise of Islam in the seventh century. Two branches are recorded by early Muslim scholars, one of which

ensuing battle with the overseeing gendarmes, many Armenians are trampled underfoot, and about a hundred women are shot.

In Edessa (Urfa)—Some of the Armenians (women and children), deported from Kharpert, Sepasdia, and their surrounding areas, are filled into a big *khan*: the one used by the local coachmen. In the cities, the gendarmes were more careful; they could not behave in an unbridled manner toward the Armenians. But, the wealthy Turks in Edessa came to agreements with the gendarmes, and entering the khan in the evenings, they would wake the women and girls and take away the most beautiful ones.

The situation was unbearable for these unfortunate souls. The difficulties of this life were so intense that mothers were obliged to make a horrific choice: that is, to sell some of their children to save the rest.

Urfa's everyday market had turned into a bazaar for selling children: the most beautiful boys were sold for ten *ghurush*.

Arap Pınar—Those who arrived in Arap Pınar were the pitiable survivors of Armenians deported from Trabzon, Samsun, Bafra, Sivas, and Amasya. They arrived after wandering for months through long winding roads: they were barefoot and hungry; their clothes were in tatters; their feet were bloodied, since there was nothing left of their shoes. The wheat that had been confiscated from the Armenian merchants in Arap Pinar remained abandoned there, on the ground. The famished deportees fell on it insatiably, devouring it with the soil and stones, like animals. The ones who ate wheat would hardly survive twenty to twenty-four hours. Their stomachs bloating, they would die, writhing in tremendous pain. Instead of preventing this, the government would, in fact, show the newcomers the fallen wheat whenever the deportees cried for bread.

The cruelty and ingenuity of the gendarmes charged with overseeing this deported population, in torturing these wretched people to death, is beyond the realm of human imagination. These gendarmes were generally chosen from among brutish Turks and Kurds from the regions of Edessa, Birecik, and Samsat. Having escaped military service, these individuals had become bandits and were being pursued as deserters. However, when the persecution of Armenians was being organized, the government declared that all those who turned themselves in would be registered as gendarmes. They would receive a post in the provinces and would be exempt from going to the front lines. These fugitives hastened to take advantage of this change in policy, and it was to these savages that the

---

resided in the northern Arabian peninsula bordering Syria and Mesopotamia.

deported population was entrusted. Officers from the Hamidian regime[10] had been assigned as the leaders of these gendarmes.

These deported people, defenseless and having been sentenced to death, were handed over to the wickedness of these devils in human form. These gendarmes had the authority to choose the manner of death for their victims according to the whims of their criminal imaginations. That is why they were unobstructed and unbridled in drawing out the Armenians' agony; this is why they subjected them to all kinds of unspeakable physical and spiritual torments; this is why they lengthened the deportees' oppressive journey and separated loved ones from one another; and this is why, after keeping the deportees hungry and thirsty for so long, they would only give them food that did not nourish them, but eventually caused them a tormenting death. They employed their menacing authority to bring forth a suffering so terrible that even the most diabolical imagination is incapable of picturing it.

Whenever they decided to send a group of these Armenians, collected from far and wide, to the bank of the Euphrates, they would arrange it so that both individuals from the same cities and villages, as well as those from the same family, were separated. They would take ten people from each city or village. Two members of a family of five would go with one group, two would go with another; then, one would remain alone, and so on. Loved ones cried and lamented as they embraced each other, not wanting to be separated, but the gendarmes would savagely pull them away from one another without feeling any sort of empathy for them.

An old woman, who had been ordered to depart alone with a group, succeeds in escaping and goes to find her daughter and daughter-in-law, so that they may all be together. By midnight, the old woman's corpse lay between the daughter and daughter-in-law. The daughter was naked and covered in blood, while the daughter-in-law's stomach had been ripped open; her intestines had fallen out from her body. She was still alive, however, and lay in agony for long hours, without anyone coming to her aid.

A conductor from Gesaria[11] recounted that a wealthy bride from Kharpert succeeded in escaping with the help of a wealthy Kurdish *bey* from Suruj. She had remained hidden beneath rocks for three days. Unable to get free and make her way to Aleppo, she eventually threw herself beneath an oncoming train.

---

[10] [MA, TMB] A reference to the tyrannical rule of Abdul Hamid, the Ottoman sultan, who founded the Hamidiye regiments out of Kurdish tribes and oppressed the Armenian community in Anatolia causing massacres and pogroms.

[11] [MA, TMB] Armenian transliteration of Kayseri.

The conductors, who were generally Christian Syrians and Greek Catholics, would collect hungry and abandoned children and bring them to Aleppo by hiding them in the coal depots. The poor little ones would understand immediately that these were their saviors and would follow them without grumbling or uttering a single whisper, so as not to give away their presence.

8

The Plain of Suruç/Suruj Plain (Armenian Cemetery). Jarābulus's Bazaar. The Image of the Nizib *Khan.*

Suruji ova (the Plain of Suruj) is a vast, flat, rocky, and arid place, where 60,000 Armenians from all parts of Armenia had been assembled. They were handed over to a group of gendarmes, who were under the supervision of a captain. Since this place was distant from the nearest city, this great multitude of women and children was deprived of aid; and death had spread among them. With the permission of the gendarmes, the surrounding Turks and Kurds incessantly went there to plunder the Armenians and to buy or steal young girls and boys. The Armenians' misery and hunger were so severe that this poor population had lost all sense of morality; they stole and sold each other's children. Many women submitted to Kurds, so that they would take them away, even as servants.

The gendarme Mahmud *Onbashi*,[1] who was an acquaintance of mine, recounted that he had made a 100 liras only by selling girls and boys. Despite his advanced age—and that he already had two wives—he also took a beautiful Armenian girl to be his wife. Turkish soldiers and gendarmes from all parts / corners of that region, leaving their work, would escape in groups and go to *Suruji ova* to take Armenian women and children away as booty. The corporal, who was leading the gendarmes at the Chifdek station, wires the captain in Jarabulus and states:

> The soldiers and the gendarmes watching the railroad at night fled to Suruj to marry. Send others.

Turks, Kurds, and other Muslims were traveling to Suruj from every corner. This, coupled with the ongoing epidemic and death occurring there, made the government uneasy. To put a stop to all this, they split the 10,000 remaining Armenians among the surrounding Kurdish villages. But refusing to feed the

---

[1] [AM] An Ottoman military title, meaning this gendarme is at the head of ten soldiers.

Armenians for free, the Kurds forced these unfortunate people to either labor for their food or marry one of them. A thousand people were lost in this manner, while the remaining few thousand were sent to Arap Punar and various other regions of Mesopotamia.

Mahmud *Onbashi* was present when the order was announced to split the remaining living population among the Kurdish villages. He was among the gendarmes overseeing those 50,000 to 60,000 Armenians.

The Armenians remained: stuck to the ground, motionless, and silent on that vast, boundless space. The gendarmes ordered everyone to stand up and immediately follow them. Groups began to stir in this motionless multitude; eventually, the gendarmes are surprised to find that hardly 10,000 people are standing. At the gendarmes' urgent commands, the Armenians begin to advance, trampling over countless corpses. The dead were spread out and piled up across the field. The few who were alive had been forced to live and sleep among the dead. They moved like gaunt, bewildered, and trembling ghosts, having lost the appearance and feeling of living human beings. They did not have the strength to walk, speak, or express anything. They moved only by instinct. Trampling over the corpses of their loved ones, they left without once turning back.

About 50,000 corpses remained unburied and rotted in the open air; *Suruji ova* became an Armenian cemetery.

And Mesopotamia's scorching sun had still not cleared that immense open-air cemetery's bones of their putrefying remains, when large new groups of half-dead Armenians began arriving successively to be subjected to the same fate. Obeying unexpected commands, only few would leave, already near death, to grow thinner on the road; and in this way, finally slowly come to nothing.

At that time, Jarābulus presented an unusual picture. The opulent and abundant plunder taken from the Armenians inhabiting the northern areas had excited the appetite of the Muslims in the southern villages. The locals grumbled that the government had been milder toward the Armenians in Cilicia, and that they had not been given free rein to plunder and massacre. Although groups of deported Armenians passed through there every day, they were famished and *lolig*,[2] having already been subjected to numerous assaults. Muslims everywhere, whether they were city-dwellers or villagers, would abandon their peaceful work and cross the Euphrates in search of fragments of the Armenian population. The question of the day was:

Are you not going to plunder the Armenians?

---

[2] [ZY] Half-naked.

Jarābulus had grown and become more prosperous. A new bazaar had opened, where many types of goods were sold daily. Row upon row of villagers, city-dwellers, functionaries, and workers came from distant places and asked—excited by avarice—where the bazaar was. Every day, the bazaar filled and emptied; both merchant and customer left extremely satisfied: the former returning home with a full purse, and the latter having appropriated very valuable objects and jewelry at a modest price. But the bazaar's goods never ran out: every day would bring new types, new models. In every Armenian-inhabited village, trade goods—jewelry, rugs, ornaments, copper and silken goods, and everything else that is rich and refined—were displayed there in a disorderly manner. It was as if Jarābulus were holding a kind of exhibit.

The customers would leave in groups and would sometimes even approach me to show what they had bought, asking:

I paid this much. Was it worth it?

The streets were full of people with varying appearances, looking festive in their new clothing. A Kurd wearing a riding coat, looks in a mirror with a sculpted frame and fixes his *kiwlah*;[3] a barefoot scoundrel wearing a velvet overcoat swaggers as he passes by; a waste-collector in silk drives out the donkeys. Here are employees who have bought rings, diamonds, gold watches, and many other ornaments, on whose faces sometimes appear Armenian letters. Jewish merchants have loaded their donkeys and camels with copperware, furnishings, home ornaments, and other goods packed onto either side of their beasts.

The surrounding villages are flooded with European goods as a result of the pillage of Armenian houses and shops. Everyone wears new clothes, new shoes, in new styles; only the *külah*s have remained constant. That half-savage population of local upstarts is flooded with the abundant wealth which the Armenians had amassed over years, through their patience and hard work, appropriating for themselves that European and Eastern industry and production.

The village mayor called me to his home to determine how much the things he had bought were worth. He showed me: rugs; shawls; silk church curtains; priests' copes embroidered with gold thread, whose crosses had been ripped out; religious vessels; and many other precious objects. Showing me a silk embroidery, he asked me with surprise:

Whose bride is this beautiful woman?

---

[3] [AM] A traditional hat, *külah* in Turkish.

It was a wrinkled handicraft, stained with streaks of dried blood, which showed Mother Armenia in chains.[4]

The Nizib khan[5] was north of Aleppo. Muslim Arab travelers sorrowfully recounted what took place within its walls. They had not seen anything with their own eyes, but they had heard fragments of stories. They had especially heard the prisoners' moving sobs and smelled the stench of corpses, which traveled quite a distance. The corporal at the *khan* would send Armenian girls as gifts to the region's wealthy inhabitants. The renown of the Armenian girls grew. Individuals praised their good breeding, their education, and their skill in fine handiworks. Thus enticed, Muslims from every corner would go there and buy women, girls, or boys, for five or ten *ghurush*.

This situation was so widely known that an official charged with overseeing the renovation of the railroad, a French Ottoman citizen, entered the Nizib *khan* on the pretext of buying a girl, and saw that dreadful sight.

This Frenchman enters the caravanserai, approaches the corporal, and asks his permission to find a woman or a girl. The corporal greets him warmly and praises the merits of Armenian women at length. He shows the Frenchman his cook and other Armenian women he has taken for himself, whose needlework adorns his room. The Frenchman expresses a desire to make his choice himself, at which point the corporal suggests that he visit the *khan*'s courtyard.

That courtyard was big and had no separate rooms; it was simply an uncovered space enclosed by four walls. At the front, and on the right side, women in rags were crowded together there, terrified and wounded. On their left side, a group of corpses had been piled up, and their stench made the air unbreathable and nauseating. The official begins to feel dizzy. Having nearly reached a drunken state, the official notices women have fallen on the newest corpses and that their cries and lamentations have been drowning out the sighs of those who are dying. Some were stripping corpses to take their clothes; some wandered around aimlessly like madmen, endlessly repeating some uniform speech or syllable. The orphaned children had gathered together there, and no one was looking after them. A freakish state dominated all of them. Not only had they forgotten one other, but it was as if they had entirely lost consciousness of themselves. The children without parents or guardians were unbelievably thin, and those tiny

---

[4] [AM] Reference to an image, popular in the nineteenth century, of a crying seated woman meant to represent Armenia. Today, a very different Soviet-era statue of "Mother Armenia," sword in hand, stands above Yerevan, Armenia's capital.

[5] [AM] *Nizibi khanĕ* in Armenian refers to a khan or caravanserai north of Aleppo in the town of Nizib (Nizip in modern Turkey).

skeletons were horrifying with their sharp feverish gazes; without a doubt, they would soon die. To postpone their agony, women were selling Kurds their sons, their clothing, and even their twelve-, thirteen-, and fourteen-year-old daughters through gaps in the walls. Often this was only for a piece of bread, which the Kurds would show the starving women as bait from a distance. The stench—together with the weeping, the groans, the guttural, almost animalistic screams, the madmen's yells, and sometimes even the horrible laughter—contributed to a hellish confusion that filled that enclosure, the sounds of which could be heard for miles.

When these unfortunate souls see a man in European clothes and understand that he has come to buy a woman, they fall upon him from every corner, hit and curse one another, wanting to make themselves seen before the foreigner. Attempting to smile on faces distorted by misery, they praised their own beauty, their merits:

> Take me, I'm beautiful, I'm such and such's daughter.

Some fortified their cases, while others refuted the stories of others:

> She lies, she lies; I was more beautiful, I was the mayor's daughter-in-law. I know how to sew, how to weave rugs. I will serve you day and night. I will be your home's dog, your prisoner, take me.

These tight rows of deportees covered in filth and feces, the deafening clamor of these proposals, with which every single woman praised her beauty, her past wealth, her family's civility and aptitude, suffocate the official. Angered, the gendarme uses his rod to rain unrelenting lashes down onto the women already afflicted with so much pain. He drove them all to their respective places, and joining his guest, began calling the women over, one-by-one, and behind to praise their plumpness, their beauty, and their health. Sometimes, he would ask:

> Whose daughter are you?

And when he heard the response, he would say:

> I know her father, he was an eminent merchant of this or that city, and was a good, rich man, and so on.

The Frenchman tours the entire caravanserai in this manner. On a rock in a corner, he suddenly notices two women who resembled each other significantly and must have been sisters. Tall, with black eyes, black hair and elegant forms, they were seated and looking ahead sadly. Although their clothes were dirty and ripped, it was clear that these had previously been costly dresses. Serious and pensive, the two women had not moved from their place. When the gendarme and the Frenchman approached them, the gendarme spoke with exceptional praise about the two women and began asking them questions:

Whose daughters are you? Where are you from?

They did not answer the questions and hopelessly looked with tear-filled eyes at the Frenchman, who was extremely moved. That hell, and seeing those noble women in that dreadful place, made him feel confused. When the women saw that the official expressed a desire to take them, they cut through the silence and asked with a desiring voice:

Are you really taking us?

The Frenchman was forced to say, *Yes!* At that point, the gendarme changes his position and begins terrorizing the Armenian women, so that they will not leave with the official:

I bought these two women, says the official, and handing over the money, he sends the gendarme away.

When the gendarme leaves them, the women quietly look at the foreigner for a long time, and the younger of the two asks him:

Sir, do you know French or English?

And they begin speaking with him in very good French.

When these women learn that the person with whom they are speaking is Christian, they implore him to somehow take them away from that hell. One of them kissed his hands, while the other clung to his feet, and their tears flowed abundantly as they begged.

Moved to an almost fatal extent, the official thought: *Where can I take them? How can I do this?* This was because he did not have a permanent home there and was forced to live with Kurds in a tent at the top of the mountain. He knew that these wretches would only be subjected to new misfortunes if he took them there. He wants to leave on his own, but the two women follow him. The gendarme does not get in their way, since he has received his payment. The two women follow the official until they reach the mountains, where he is obliged to take them to a nearby Kurdish village. He hands the Armenians over to the village's mayor and pays him a few months' living expense, so that they might be comfortable and safe with the mayor.

These women were from the environs of Gesaria.

9

The Transportation of the Population by Train. Water . . . Water . . . A Woman from Yerznga, and the Deportation of Yerznga. The Story of Chemeshgadzak.

From April to November 1915, trains arrived in Jarābulus full of Armenians deported from Resulayn, Tele Abyad, and Arap Pınar. These were multitudes of women, girls, and boys, all of them hopeless, all their eyelids bloodied, their faces flooded with tears. Only those with money were able to ride in the passenger cars.

A Greek acquaintance of mine, who was traveling to Aleppo with a train transporting Armenians, showed me a girl in a black velvet dress and said:

> Brother, a pretty, pure girl like this, who speaks good French, had fallen into the hands of the Kurds. I was hardly able to free her with the help of a soldier friend of mine, saying that I was going to take her as my wife.

The girl's mother, hearing me speak Armenian, called me over. I went to them and learned that they were from Amasia. Through sighs of grief and pain, tears flowing from their eyes, they explained that they were members of a wealthy family. The mother asked me, pointing to the young Greek man, whether he was really Christian:

> Promise me that you'll give my daughter to him as his wife, she said, because he saved us from the hands of those beasts.

There were ten more Armenian women in the same car, but I could not find two people from the same city. The deported population had been separated, such that among those ten, there were women from Bapron, Gerason, Samsak, Yerrznga, Sepasdia,[1] and other places, each person from a different place.

---

[1] [MA, TMB] Armenian versions of place names of Samsun, Giresun, Samsak, Erzincan, and Sivas.

They were all overburdened with grief, longing, and bitterness. Nevertheless, they told me of the painful difficulties they had met in the stations, where even Christian officials had ruthlessly exploited their ignorance, terror, and panic. These officials would not sell the Armenians tickets until they paid double, triple, and sometimes even more than the original price. Hundreds of Turkish soldiers would crowd around the cars of Armenian refugees and sell them bread worth five *paras*[2] for two or three *ghurush*. Often, when they noticed a woman's or a girl's trembling hand extended to buy their bread, they would say to each other:

> Ah, if we were allowed, each of us would have taken one of these women for himself.

On those trains, I met my relatives among the Armenians there: the Zerderian family from Dikranagerd, who were wealthy merchants, as well as the wife and daughters of Mr. Sukeasian, the director of Chemeshgadzak's agricultural bank. Being in a state of desperate need, these two women had been reduced to begging for a piece of bread and a few *ghurush* to spend on the road. It was difficult to recognize them at first glance; they had lost their beauty and grace, and appeared grotesque and miserable, yellow and blue from fear, and blackened by the sun.

In every station, the Armenian exiles were subjected to all kinds of torments and affronts. The soldiers assigned to protect these stations felt unruly in their impudence. The water pump was always on the right side of the station, while the left side was always wild and deserted. When a train would stop, one group of exiles would run, parched, to the water source, while another group would go to the left side to relieve themselves. The soldiers, lying in wait in ditches, would suddenly assault these poor women, and they dared to rape them even in the major stations. On the other side, by the water source, Turks would similarly move freely among the gathered girls and boys. A shriek would suddenly rise out of the crowd, while others would cry out loudly or uselessly beg for aid.

Having been the targets of such dishonors, these unfortunate women would often take refuge in the rail cars without quenching their thirst. Groups of crowded children were trampled underfoot, or the water they obtained with great difficulty would spill, and their poor parched lips would continue longing for water. They were so tormented by thirst that they would sometimes fall to the floor and lap up the water that had spilled from the well and had already gone underfoot.

---

[2] [TN] Ottoman unit of currency, smaller than a *kuruş*.

Seeing this day after day, a friend and I decided to find some sort of solution. We gathered a few Arab boys and arranged the distribution of bread, and especially that of water, to the Armenian deportees arriving at our station.

As soon as a train would stop, we would approach the cars with pails of water and bread. Afraid of the soldiers at the station, most of the deportees would not deboard, but would rather reach out with their vessels so that we could fill them. If the vessel was copper, the soldiers would snatch it and flee. However, copper vessels were an exception; in general, they had only rusty tin vessels, dried pumpkins, and empty bottles left by the Germans. And these were the lucky ones—the majority remained without any means of carrying water. The extreme heat had made them seem possessed. They would shout out incomprehensibly and hoarsely through dry lips and contorted tongues. As soon as it was possible, thousands of arms would reach out, and the deportees would cry out, *water . . . water . . .*

The government did not look favorably on the aid we were giving the Armenians, which, in comparison with their misery, was very little. Nevertheless, we paid no heed to their threatening looks; every time we would approach the cars, each of us would carry two large vessels of water. The exiles were generally crowded into the baggage cars, which had four small windows and two doors shut from the outside. When I would approach a car and open one of the doors, a group of people would crowd it. As if wanting to flee a hell, they would rush upon me and rain curses down on me from all sides, believing me to be the one who had locked them there. These unfortunate ones / these unfortunate souls had no room to sit, and they crawled about like worms. Innumerable mouths demanded one thing: *water . . . water . . .* Some, throwing caution to the wind, would throw themselves out of the cars and go to the water pump.

Distributing water in an orderly fashion to that impatient, parched, and bewildered multitude proved impossible, and half the water would fall uselessly to the ground. They would push each other and try to steal the vessels from each other's hands. Swearing and malediction thundered in the cars whenever trembling or cramped hands turned a vessel over, spilling the water and wetting the people's rags. At that point, the children would silently cling to the women's clothes so they could suck the water off the wet fabric.

Compassion for one another, even among relatives, had disappeared entirely.

Extremely agitated by the torments they had borne, everyone looked at the other deportees as enemies. Hunger and thirst had made them mad and insatiable. They had the manner of wild beasts, and it often occurred that women grasped at each other's throats for a glass of water. Fights, insults, and a thousand curses over a single glass of water were incessant. The strong would win, while the weak would be left helpless, defeated by even their own relatives.

The distribution of bread was even more difficult. I was unable to give each individual their share, because as soon as I would enter a car, the deportees would assail me and scratch at my hands to snatch away the bread. As a result, I was forced to throw the bread from a distance, and I would turn my eyes away so as not to see the horrible and silent struggle taking place wherever it fell.

Once, two women from the same village were standing with their children at a train's last car, which was used to transport sheep. They were barefoot, and their rags hardly covered their bodies. The bread I had brought with me was finished, but they begged me for something to eat, beseeching me with heart-rending pleas. Pressed, I found some pieces of dry bread; and wrapping them in a handkerchief, I threw the package over to the women. They immediately ran toward it, while their children crawled after them. I saw them for an instant: their faces blackened by the sun, their fangs bared, their hollow eyes lit by a wild and panicked passion as they prepared for an unrelenting struggle. A major fight ensued: they struggled with sharp and hasty movements, without speaking, and their children trembled as they watched, astonished by their mothers. One of them finally won and hurled the other to the ground. The children went crying toward their respective mothers. Meanwhile, the victorious woman, having taken the dried bread, ripped open the handkerchief without waiting to untie it. The woman began eating furiously and gave only one piece to her beseeching children.

In the cars, there were also children whose mothers had died during the journey. These helpless orphans would remain crowded together to one side, and amid the general confusion, they would not dare to come forward to drink water. The other women, who had forgotten even their own children, did not care for these unfortunate souls at all. The railroad company's telegrams informed us almost daily that ten to twelve children had died of thirst. And these trains passed through stations where there had been great ease in distributing water.

It must be noted also that this miserable and blunted crowd had once been once part of a wealthy, educated, and refined population. They were mostly from cities, and familial love, as well as caring and sacrifice for one another, had made up their greatest virtues. Long-lasting and unheard-of misfortunes had distorted not only their physical appearances but also their souls, and they had become animal-like creatures deprived of all human feeling, clinging desperately to life. Within each and every one of them, a single feeling, a single fear now reigned: hunger and thirst.

Once, when I opened a car door to distribute some water, a woman with a horrifying look appeared before me. Everyone was afraid of her and had moved away, leaving the area around her empty. When they saw me, some of the exiled ones implored me to take her away, saying that she was violently mad.

The woman looked everyone over with her sharp and menacing gaze. Throwing her knotted hair back from over her face and raising the pail of water to her mouth, she began drinking insatiably. Then she said, looking at me:

I'm not mad, brother.
Although the water was freezing cold, it did not quench her thirst, and she complained: "This is hot, bring me some cold water."

When she was sufficiently relaxed, her head moved convulsively as she repeated:

I am Kevork Agha's daughter; I'm not mad.

Her hands were completely bloodied, and she contracted her fingers as if to dispel something imaginary. Even the Turkish soldiers could not withstand her ferocious expression and ran away fearfully.

The Christian railroad officials, all from different backgrounds, were profoundly affected by these images of misery unfolding daily before their eyes. Regardless, their compassion could not make any fundamental change. Whenever they met girls or boys on the open fields—who had stayed behind, had been forgotten, or had fled—they would keep them hidden from the government in trunks or beneath supplies and would transport them to Aleppo. This was how a fifteen-year-old boy from Sepasdia passed through Jarābulus. He wore girls' clothes, and he was the only boy from Armenia whom I met among that endless, passing multitude. When he realized that I had discovered his disguise, he fearfully begged me not to reveal it to anyone.

A train made up of forty cars arrived in Jarābulus almost entirely empty. Visiting the train, I met a woman from Erznga and asked her

How is it that they left you alone and you're traveling alone?

She was intensely moved by hearing Armenian, and she began to weep. Then she began her story:

I was able to keep one of my daughters with me, who was very beautiful, as we traveled from Erznga to Arap Punar, by paying substantial bribes to everyone. In Arap Punar, a Christian German engineer was very pleased with my daughter, and he said that there wasn't any difference between Armenians and Germans, since they are both Christians. He convinced me and took my daughter, saying that he would marry her. He also ordered them to bring me safely to Aleppo, promising me that in two or three days, he would also come, and that they would marry in Aleppo. I suggested that my daughter stay with me, but he said, No, it's better that she stay with me and become accustomed to my character and language.

This same woman also recounted the deportation from Erznga in the following manner:

> The government gave the Armenians twenty-four hours, after which everyone would have to leave the city. A feeling of desperation dominated there; but even when the people first appealed, it became clear that the order was final, and that the government would not yield for anyone. At that point, all the citizens prepared themselves, and every one of them brought a part of their monetary or gold riches with them. Goods in commercial houses, wealth credited and owed, movable and immovable: everything fell into the hands of the enemy.
>
> The principal of the school and his wife, along with another wealthy person from Erznga, understood what awaited them and poisoned themselves.
>
> When the twenty-four hours were up, the entire Armenian population, men and women both, was assembled and sent out onto the road. In the beginning, the gendarmes for the most part behaved themselves; they pretended that their supervision was serious and strict. But when we arrived at Kemakhi Boghaz,[3] the gendarmes' attitude suddenly changed. An officer and his gendarmes began collecting the riches that the deportees had brought with them. 50,000 liras, in cash, and a pile of finery were handed over to the soldiers, who took all this in accordance with the instructions they had received. The plundered Armenians, disheartened and sensing the new misfortunes that awaited them, emerged from the boghaz (gorge) and were suddenly face-to-face with a Kurdish mob. The population was immediately separated. The men, who were entirely unarmed, were guided to a nearby hill, where the gendarmes began ruthlessly massacring them by crushing their skulls with cudgels and rocks. The heart-wrenching cries of the dying men were all around us; the sounds of our desperate and powerless fury resounded and sometimes even drowned out the tumult of those brutal blows. Women and girls cried, screamed, wanting to go to their relatives; their loved ones were being massacred, but the gendarmes overpowered them with blows from their rods; blood often flowed with tears down the faces of the wounded.
>
> A crowd of Kurds, having finished their morning work, came at midday to a group of women. When they had chosen the beautiful girls and taken those ones

---

[3] [AM] Gorge that spans the Euphrates, which was a common site of massacre during the genocide.

away, the gendarmes led us to a big spring but then forbade us from approaching the water. We were thirsty; we were burnt; but it was impossible to go to the spring. We had lost our minds, and our hearts were bleeding. We gathered close together and cried from desperation and pain right under the pitiless eyes of the gendarmes, who mocked our pain and derided us. After waiting in this state until evening, we were forced to bring forth our hidden money and finery as bribes for the gendarmes, who only allowed us to drink after paying them.

Every evening, the gendarmes would demand one virgin girl from the group. If we did not hand one over, they would keep us thirsty and make us walk without rest. Consumed by thirst and exhaustion, we would ask for a break or some water; they would repeat their demand and would not budge until they were satisfied.

It was under these conditions that we completed our journey from Erznga to Samsat, during which time children and older women died incessantly from thirst or hunger. Seeing our group, Kurds and Turks would run to us and, paying a few ghurush to the overseeing gendarmes, would take girls and brides as their own.

We reached Samsat and stayed there for one full day. The local Turks would enter our group unobstructed and take boys and girls either by force or for money, such that, when we arrived in Arap Punar, there were no longer any girls among us.

On another day, a woman from Chemeshgadzak in a railcar recounted the following:

A Kurdish bey sent us seventy mules and gave word that the Turkish government was to massacre us. And so, he proposed: "Whoever is able should come by mule or on foot and take refuge with me." The Armenian residents of our region's four villages fled in their entirety to the bey. We could not respond to that invitation because the government's gendarmes had arrived already. They gathered us with haste and took us away. They sent the men to Kharpert and brought us to Arap Pınar on foot, via long and difficult roads through the mountains.

Having traveled over the same road as the Armenian population from Erznga, these exiled people had suffered similar tribulations.

When the Turkish women found out that Armenians from Armenia were to pass through the Jarābulus train station, they would come down in groups and curse at the poor Armenians with unspeakable and shameful phrases. They would say that their sons had been killed by Armenian bullets in Armenia's fields, and that the Armenians were the cause of their current troubles. They would approach the cars—and despite the deported women's wretched and miserable appearance—they would hurl all range of insults at them, all the while spitting on them and stoning them. Turkish women have even entered the cars and choked an Armenian woman or child. Their hatred was so intense that they would often succeed in inciting the Muslims against the local peaceful Armenians.

An Armenian doctor, who was returning from Resulayn under a Turkish name, explained that from Zifteg to Resulayn, a distance of 180 kilometers, both sides of the line were piled with the corpses of Armenian women and children. Meanwhile, the tracks in the stations had been entirely covered in blood. In many places, the blood that had pooled in the triangular spaces where two sets of tracks meet had by then congealed.

Foreigners and German soldiers saw all this. Curious about the horrible scenes unfolding every day in the stations, women would come and photograph what they saw, and, getting even more than they had hoped for, they would return content.

10

The Deported Population on Foot Toward Aleppo. A Bride's Escape. The Passage of Seventy Armenians from Erzrum (the Deportation of Erzrum).

A bride from Anchrti[1] village in the region of Arapgir recounted the following:

On Friday, we boiled the red egg,[2] but we couldn't eat it Saturday evening. They deported us from our village the same day; and on the road, they massacred, plundered, and took the women and girls away. A Kurd took me, but I succeeded in tricking him, fleeing at night. I returned to our village where there were no longer any Armenians. Wandering around the region for a few days, I found my relatives and acquaintances among the Kurds; and meeting with them secretly, I exhorted them to take the risk and escape with me. Three young women joined me, and we set off together for Aleppo.[3] Sleeping in the mountains at night and moving through the valleys by day, we advanced slowly: alone, helpless, and hungry. Guards were stationed everywhere, and even the most insignificant passes were guarded by a small guardhouse, such that we were always forced to take long detours and wander for one or two days to avoid being seen. To safeguard our honor and our freedom, we had forgotten pain, hunger, exhaustion, and all kinds of suffering. Sometimes, we would fall: spent, onto the dry soil, our legs bloody and swollen; and we would groan from exhaustion. At times we thought we would never be able to rise again; hunger forced us to look for grass, since that was our only nourishment. But thirst was our greatest torment: fatigue, heat, and eating grass made us so thirsty that our parched tongues grew heavy in our mouths, and we could not move our dry and cut lips to talk to each other. We searched for water with silent and hasty movements; and climbing to

---

[1] [MA, TMB] Present-day Topkapı, one of the villages of Arapgir.
[2] [TN] Eggs painted red for Easter.
[3] [ZY] It is a journey of approximately 400 kilometers to Aleppo.

the tops of hills, we would peer out over the dry landscape and run immediately to pools of water whenever we would see them.

Once, we came across a stagnant pond. The earth around it was dry and cracked, while its shore was a slippery mud; it was as such because if someone tried to approach the pond, they would be up to their knees in mud and would hardly be able to free themselves without going toward the water. One of our friends was suffering from thirst so much that despite our warnings, she threw herself into the water, and was unable to find her footing; she sank in the thick mud beneath the water's surface. A Kurd was passing by on a distant road. Desperate, we called him over; he immediately came and boldly jumped into the water, saving our friend. We were so thirsty that we did not concern ourselves very long with our friend's condition, and wringing out her wet skirt, we insatiably sucked the filthy water.

We heard that some wealthy Armenians had arrived near Birecik on four rafts over the Euphrates, and that they had chosen to rest on an open field. I (H. Toroyan) went to them and saw the following: sixty women and children and ten men were sitting dispersed in a cavity in the sand on the riverbank. Among those people were several members of notable families, who were acquaintances of mine; they were all sitting there, gnawing at pieces of watermelon. They had received special permission from the government to reach Aleppo, because the brother of one of the notables from Erzrum was a high-ranking government official there, and he had succeeded in saving his brother and their extended family. The person, heading that group from Erzrum, recounted the following:

In Erzrum, the government gave us a ten-day timeframe within which to leave the city.[4] In that period, the Turks behaved very affably toward us; and to further deceive us, they would not even allow us to sell our goods at lower prices, claiming our situation was temporary and that we would soon return to our city. They encouraged us, made promises, and feigning a sort of sweetness toward us, they strove to make it so that we would not understand what was about to befall us. Nevertheless, the Armenians organized a meeting and conferred on what course of action to take. The young people suggested disobeying the government's order and even insisted that we needed to resist and remain in our homes, to fight if necessary. But those who were older and wealthier were opposed to violent means. They preferred to submit to the government's order, believing that the Armenian population would be saved this way. They believed

---

[4] [ZY] Here, we omit the details of several events, which can be found in more complete detail in other works.

that disobedience, especially through violent resistance, would be the most catastrophic course of action for everyone. Those preaching caution won the majority, and the Armenians from Erzrum decided to be deported without showing any resistance.

Once the ten days were over, we rented carts, horses, donkeys, and mules with the government's help and loaded them with our valuable possessions, along with a trivial portion of our wealth. On the eleventh day, we set out from our native city for Erznga, accompanied by a *kaymakam* and 100 soldiers meant to defend us. In order to express their respect to the departing population, the high-ranking government officials came as a group all the way to the gates of Erzrum to bid us farewell; they sent us off with all due civility.

It was difficult and painful to leave our homes, to leave our wealth, and just go, even temporarily; but the attitude of the Turks at the time, even up to the last moment, made it so that we did not have the slightest suspicion of the horrible events that were prescribed for us. From Erzrum to Erznga, the *kaymakam* and soldiers accompanying us behaved with the utmost respect; the soldiers would not even approach the groups of women but rather walked at a distance. When we approached Paypert,[5] we saw two to three fallen corpses in the field, but we again did not think this was a crime committed by the Turks. In this way, we arrived near Erznga, where the convoy stopped in an open field. A few acquaintances and I went into the city of Erznga to put our affairs in order and to rent a house or a room for our families. But when I entered Erznga, a feeling of astonishment and dread came over me: the Armenian market was empty; the houses were open and empty; and the entire city was deserted. Not a single Armenian remained. Confused, agitated, I went to see the governor, but he avoided answering my questions and immediately informed me that he had received orders from Aleppo to transport my family and I safely to Aleppo, under the protection of gendarmes. I realized everything at that point; I suddenly comprehended the misfortune that had befallen us. I wanted to hastily leave, but the governor insisted that I wait for the gendarmes assigned to protect me, because from then on, every Armenian would be in danger. Soon thereafter, I arrived at the field where the Armenians from Erzrum had stopped, and at a single glance, I saw what was a horrific scene. The *kaymakam* and soldiers who had accompanied us from Erzrum had disappeared, and the field was covered with a mob of Kurds, Turks, and soldiers, who were there among the defenseless population: they were plundering, massacring, and taking anyone who came

---

[5] [MA, TMB] Modern day Bayburt, a city in northeast Turkey lying on the Chorokh (*Çoruh*) river.

across their paths. Shrieks, screams, and cries of pain and desperation were among the enemy's curses and derision. I was hardly able to save my family and a few friends with the help of the gendarmes, while the remaining thousands became scattered. Many had been trampled underfoot; children and old women, clinging to their slaughtered loved ones, cried and screamed; thousands of corpses littered the field, having received a fatal wound to the head or stomach, or having been killed in any number of horrible manners. A small part of that great multitude became scattered all over those mountains and fields, having lost each other in a maddened state. The caravan to which I had given my silk packs and my other valuable possessions had likewise disappeared.

In the middle of this confusion, a group of Armenian deportees from Drabizon arrived; among them were two notable merchants. They came and joined me, as members of my family, and without pausing, we assembled our small caravan and set off for Kemakh. There, in the Kemakh gorge, a soldier took my first-born son, twenty-eight years old, and his friend. Despite my supplications and my promises, he wouldn't hand my son over to me. I promised him up to 20,000 liras, but the soldier remained unmoved. So we were forced to leave our first-born son; and grieving, we moved on to Malatia; I wanted to get some money from the local branch there, but the city was entirely empty. There were no Armenians left here either, and in my rashness, I myself nearly became a victim.

We continued our journey and stopped in a nearby village to spend the night. One of the local begs[6] approached our group; after searching for a long time, he set his sights on the Kavafians' new daughter-in-law. The gendarmes who were with us tried to defend the young girl, but the beg grew angry at that resistance and threatened to wipe out our entire group if the woman were not handed over to him. She had lost her parents, her husband, and nearly her entire family and was in a state of deep despair. Seeing that the quarrel over her could become dangerous, she submitted herself willingly to the beg, in order to save our group.

Kavafian was one of Erzrum's wealthy merchants, and he had given the government 20,000 liras worth of sugar, coffee, and money. He had paid his three sons' bedel[7] and had worked to facilitate and regulate the provisioning of the military. Nonetheless, they had murdered his wife and three sons in front of his very eyes, and unable to withstand his grief, he too died suddenly in Erznga.

We arrived in Samsat, where we stayed for three days. All the Armenians had been driven out from Samsat too; only a few Armenian women remained

---

[6] [AM] Turkish title, the root of "bey," similar to chief, gentleman, mister.
[7] [MA, TMB] The word "bedel" has a number of meanings in Turkish which include: "price," "worth," "compensation," "to pay a price for something," "to pay the penalty for," as such.

there, and they worked as slaves in the market's kebab restaurants and coffee houses. I met a shepherd who had an Armenian wife and two Armenian maidservants. Considering me a knowledgeable person, people would show me tin-plated bowls filled with gold rings and other jewelry, which they were selling at extremely low prices. Thousands of rugs and many other valuable objects were heaped up in the bazaar. Everyone had grown haughty and insolent, even the *gendarmes* who were accompanying us. Whenever I offered them a hundred liras in exchange for a small service, they wouldn't accept it, saying that it was too little.

11

Groups of Armenians Passing through Birecik. Murad, Murad,[1] You Have Fulfilled Our Wishes.

About 20,000 Armenians, women and children, who had been deported from various places, but especially from Erzrum and Kharpert, were transferred from Edessa (Urfa) to Birecik on the government's orders. The Turks here, who hated the Armenians intensely and were waiting for an opportunity like this, fell upon the Armenians, saying: *These are our prisoners, the people fighting against us*; they began plundering and kidnapping the women and girls. Every Turk took a girl or woman. They even took girls as young as twelve as wives. Old women would come and take girls for their absent sons as a means of *sevab* (acceptable to God).[2] The Turkish population was allowed to conduct itself in any manner it wished, and the Armenian deportees were subjected to these whims, without any means of defending themselves against all these manners of dishonor. One of my acquaintances, Hasan Effendi, who was a fifty-year-old man, said to me without embarrassment:

> There was a fifteen-year-old girl, very pretty. I tried so hard to convince her to marry me willingly, but she rejected me. I felt sorry for her and did not want to take her by force, so I gave her to my brother, who is ten years younger than me.

The exiled Armenians remained in that field in Birecik for two weeks. There were neither girls nor boys with them any longer, because not only the locals but also the mayors of the surrounding villages had come and taken their share of both girls and boys, with the government's blessing. There remained only old

---

[1] [ZY] The local Muslim population sometimes calls the Euphrates *Murad*, which means "wish" in Turkish. [AM]: In the original, this is written as "Murad, Murad, you have fulfilled all our murads [wishes]."

[2] [MA, TMB] *sevap*, from Ottoman Turkish *sevāb* means "divine reward" for a good dead. The word comes from Arabic *ṭawāb* meaning "reward," especially one that accrues from one's good deeds or piety.

women and sick children, who died, one by one; in this way, this group of 20,000 deportees was wiped out.

An Armenian woman named Karajian—who had fallen into the hands of Turks in one of the villages surrounding Birecik—hearing that there were Armenians nearby, had succeeded in sending the following note:

> My daughter and I are alive. My husband lives in America. Please write to him and ask him to come save us. We are in a state of unbearable need, please send us money.

A ten-year-old Kurdish child spoke of the Armenian women in his village in the following manner:

> They wash themselves every day, uselessly, and use a lot of water. They don't want to sit next to us. They say, "You're dirty, you smell." They don't eat the bread we give them, saying it's dry. They say, "We used to eat well in our country."

I asked a Kurd:

> Boy, why do you give them dry bread?

He replied:

> My father gives them dry bread on purpose, so that they'll die.

Growing increasingly provoked, he added:

> We wanted this geavur[3] woman's daughter for my brother, but they wouldn't give her to us.[4] How are we supposed to give them soft bread after that? But they have a younger daughter who is my age, who tells really good stories. I like that little girl a lot.

I was sitting in my room, when I heard the Turks shouting:

> "*Yesir gelyor, yesir, yesir!*"[5] (Prisoners are coming, prisoners, prisoners!)

The Turks either called the Armenians *yesir* or *muhajir* (prisoner or refugee).

It was noon and intensely hot: the sun was so scorching that the birds hid in the shade beneath rocks. The thermometer in my room read forty-two.[6] Despite

---

[3] [MA, TMB] Armenian transliteration of the Turkish word *gâvur*, which comes from the Arabic term *kâfir* meaning someone who is a disbeliever in God and the Islamic faith. The term can be translated simply as "infidel" and was used as a slur for non-Muslims, mostly Christians, across the Ottoman Empire.
[4] [MA, TMB] Here the reference is to giving the girl as a wife to the speaker's brother.
[5] [MA, TMB] The remark in Turkish should be "*Esir geliyor, esir, esir!*"
[6] [AM] Degrees Celsius.

how hot it was, they made the exiles walk. Curious, I ran outside and, joining the Turks, I went to meet the Armenians.

A group of more than 600 people was coming down a hill toward a vast sandy field. They were not walking; they were tumbling. When they saw the Euphrates, they changed their course toward the water. The children hastened toward the water as well, hanging from their mother's skirts so as not to fall behind. There were pregnant women who, although they were parched, could not walk and sat there on the sand. Old women, preparing their skins, moved toward the water. Adolescents and children ran to the river, mad and panting. It was as if that miserable, hungry, and thirsty crowd, having felt the bitter horror of death, was running toward life . . . all this: despite the fact that the banks of the Euphrates were still covered with corpses, and that the water had been corrupted by those corpses' putrefaction.

About seven, eight barefoot boys and girls had remained behind the group; they were limping and crying, their feet burning in the sand.

Seeing that the deportees were moving toward the water, the gendarmes whipped their horses to catch up with the group. Once they reached them, the gendarmes began screaming, bellowing, and whipping them; then, they succeeded in turning the exiled ones back. The weeping and lamentation, the entreaties, cursing of the gendarmes, and the cracks of whips altogether filled up the entire place. And the Armenians, dying of thirst, passed before us without approaching the water. At that moment, they were silent: they were all hopeless, their eyes wandering, their faces disfigured, torn from the lashes of the whips. No sound, no cry could be heard; there was only the muffled sound of the sand, warmed by the sun as it was rustling under bare feet; or the children, encouraged by the gendarmes' distance from the convoy, pointing at the river and imploring their mothers for water.

The deportees left two corpses on the road: a pregnant woman and a child. The corpses remained there unburied. On the second day, we sent a Turk to go and bury them, paying him a substantial sum. When he returned, he said the corpses were naked: the villagers had looted their rags, as they always did.

The gendarmes' corporal brought up the rear of the caravan, and the Turkish bystanders gathered around him. Among this crowd was the Armenophobic Hoja Oghli, who, speaking to the corporal, said:

> *Berader*[7] (brother), *why do you tire yourself with those bitches? When they don't obey, throw them into the river.*

---

[7] [MA, TMB] The correct form of brother in Turkish should be *birader*.

Then he added, excited:

> Janem, the sevdii Murad (the very dear Murad River) takes so many of these corpses every day.

From a distance, someone else exclaimed:

> Oh Murad, Murad! You have fulfilled our Murad!"

The corporal smiled and laughed demonically, and said:

> I am all-powerful, I have authority over life and death. Of these 600 people, not even 6 will remain. . . . But why rush? Slowly, slowly, the time has not yet come. In a month's time, you will see how many of them will remain.

12

Aleppo. Turkish and Armenian Committees for Settling the Deportees. The Behavior of Aleppo's Armenian Population. The Condition of Aleppo's Armenian Population. A General Picture. The Passage of the Armenian Intellectuals. Zohrab and Vartkes.

Aleppo is a wealthy commercial city with a population of about 450,000, of whom 18,000 are Armenian. There are a small number of Jews, but Christian and Muslim Arabs make up the vast majority of the city's inhabitants. The number of Turks is small and is comprised of officials and soldiers.

The Armenian populace is made up as such: high hundred homes of local Armenians, who are Arabic speakers and even read the Gospels in Arabic; and 1,200 homes of Armenians who immigrated to Aleppo a long time ago from different villages and who are Armenian speakers.

After the proclamation of the Ottoman constitution, the intellectual and economic conditions of the Armenians improved quickly. At the people's initiative, along with that of various political parties, auditoriums and theaters were opened, as well as a meeting house, where debates took place on matters of education and literature. Kindergartens were opened at the expense of the wealthy merchant Levon Bey Ajemian. The Aleppo Armenians had coed schools, whose programs were crafted in accordance with the demands of modern life. National musical troupes were formed, as well as a girls' library and a women's patriotic association. Partisan weekly collotypes were also published. There were plans to organize a printing press and publish a daily newspaper, but the war put a stop to these.

Goods from all over Armenia were concentrated in Aleppo, such as skins, gum, gall-nuts, wool, animal intestines, almonds, walnuts, and oil. Aleppo's market, which was mostly in the hands of Armenians, had an important place in city life. The work of importing foreign goods to the interior, which had formerly been done by Jews, passed into the hands of Armenians, who opened large store-houses. The banks, especially Deutsche Orientbank, gave the Armenians substantial loans. The German railroad employees, contract workers, and doctors were almost all Armenian, and so too were a portion of its surveyors.

Almost all of Aleppo's doctors and pharmacists were Armenian, and many had their own personal hospitals. Most of the artisans, especially those who worked on fine handicrafts, were also Armenian.

In Aleppo, there was a German elementary school; a Latin college, where students can board and which is the main school for Aleppo's Christians; a school for girls run by French Sisters, where orphans from Adana are educated; as well as the Armenian Catholic kindergarten. Armenian boys and girls make up a big number of the students in these foreign schools.

A notable and trustworthy resident of Aleppo recounted the following:

The deportation of Cilicia began in April 1915. The government ordered a committee established for settling the arriving refugees, finding them homes, caravanserais, and so on, as well as furnishing them with their daily food (only providing them with flour). The local Armenians took care of everything else. The Turkish committee informed the Armenians every day of the arrival of deportees, while also reporting which direction they were coming from, in what numbers, and so on. The refugees from Cilicia were settled sufficiently well, and both men and women went on to do different kinds of work in the markets. Their economic situation was stable, especially since they had been subjected to little plunder; and so, they had been able to bring a portion of their funds with them. Since Aleppo was near their homeland and its climate similar to theirs, the situation of these deportees was favorable, compared to others.

We were informed that deportees from Armenia were arriving. The local Armenians went to greet them, and the first meeting took place on a road outside the city. They were a crowd of about 2,000 women and children, not a single man among them. Emaciated, blackened by the sun, covered in rags, hungry and thirsty: they looked as if they were possessed. So much dust had blown onto their faces, that from a distance, they looked like a single, earth-colored mass that had been stuck together and was now almost inseparable. They stood motionless, not knowing where they were to go or what they were to do. They could neither protest, nor speak—they were silent. Sometimes, a woman would shake her head as she sighed from weariness or pain, or a child would fall from exhaustion. And they waited there in that state. For an instant, we doubted that these were the ones we were looking for, but when we realized that these unfortunate ones were Armenians, we became, like them, stunned. We could neither walk nor speak; we stood face-to-face with them in a silent pain. This is how our first meeting with Armenians from Armenia took place.

Finally emerging from our dumbfounded state, we led the exiles to the Armenian Church. On the road, Turks, Kurds, Arabs, and half-savage Bedouins all watched us in astonishment and said to one another, "Are there really people like this in our country?" Only the Arab sheikhs understood everything and exclaimed each time:

Suppan Allah alehel zılım[1]! (Glory be to God, what kind of an oppression is this?)

After that first arrival of Armenian deportees, the Turkish committee notified us daily of the arrival of any new group, either by train or on foot. The deportees arrived in successively worse conditions. Emaciated, in a vegetative state, many close to death; they had all lost any sort of human appearance. About 70,000 deported Armenians were settled in Aleppo; these groups had come from different places, the remnants of big and prosperous cities. Women and children, who had not been able to keep their families together, arrived from Bafra, Drabizon, Erzrum, Dikranagerd, and these cities' environs, since every family was divided among the groups going to different places.

The local Armenians organized the relief effort with great fervor and devotion: the doctors, led by Dr. Samuel Shmavonian (president of the Benevolent Society),[2] visited the sick without respite. Dr. Shmavonian became such a visible figure through his personal efforts and sacrifices that the government took him into custody. He was released a few days later thanks to the interventions of influential people. Taking up his former role once again, he became infected with a contagious disease and died. A women's organization also played an important role. These women, through their own efforts, almost singlehandedly protected and comforted those 70,000 exiles. They personally prepared meals for the deportees, when needed, begging from one street to the other, for clothes and provisions—their devotion knowing no limits. The efforts of all these individuals, in addition to the small amount of aid provided by the government, considerably softened the deportees' situation. A medical group was established under the supervision of Dr. Samuel, and a group of adolescents and young adults

---

[1] [MA, TMB] The phrase is transliterated here according to Yesayan's Armenian. This glorifying phrase or *tasbīḥ*, *Subḥān-Allāh*, can be translated as "Glory be to Allāh" or "Allāh is perfect." The Turkish word *zulüm* means "oppression" or "atrocity" rather than catastrophe. The word is derived from the Arabic *ẓulm* used to describe injustice, wrongdoing, or oppression.

[2] [AM] Dr. Shmavonian was a leading figure in the Aleppo branch of the Armenian General Benevolent Union (AGBU), which was founded in 1906 in Cairo, and which still exists today.

was also formed under another individual's direction. This latter group worked day and night with the aforementioned women, helping to settle the deportees: to wash, clean, heal, and feed them, and whenever possible, to procure work for those who were willing and able. Aleppo's Armenian population generally welcomed it's unfortunate fellow Armenians with open arms: they opened their doors to the refugees; and everyone sheltered five to ten of these exiled people in their homes, whether these were acquaintances of theirs or not. Nevertheless, the city's streets, fields, and unfamiliar corners were crowded with thousands of homeless and unfortunate souls. The church's district presented an especially unbearable picture. The roads were crowded and closed, and the deportees slept on the streets right next to their excrements. Walking among these exiles was impossible and coming to their aid was difficult in the extreme. Although part of the homeless population had been settled in national properties—caravanserais, schools, the attic of the church, everywhere—the crowding of those unfortunates resulted in many deaths and the disappearance of many boys and girls.

The government gradually halted its aid and changed its policies. They searched the homes of local Armenians, and although they found nothing suspicious, they nonetheless arrested those who were aiding the exiles, some of the wealthy locals, and me. This was a mere formality, a kind of warning, and we were released twenty-four hours later.

At the same time, the government declared that any exiled women, girls, boys, and so on who were being sheltered by local Armenians needed to be sent away. Any local who did not comply with this order would be deported themselves and become exiled.

Fear reigned over the local population: the forces aiding the deportees became unnerved, and everyone feared publicly helping them. The aid given clandestinely was insufficient. The exiled Armenians remained helpless: hunger, illness, and misery made the number of deaths grow daily, until it reached a hundred deaths per day. The situation was so dire that even foreigners began protesting. For example, the wife of a German official, Mrs. Kokh, who helped the Armenians swarming around her home, protested to the government, saying that innocent Armenians confined in rooms or courtyards around their home were dying from starvation.

To get ahead of these complaints and complications, the government had begun sending the poor refugees in the streets, in groups, to the surrounding area and to Mesopotamia.

With the hope of finding a remedy to this horrible situation, I went to the commander of the army in Syria and Egypt, Jemal Pasha, and received the following reply: *What is happening here is very little compared with the cruelties committed by Armenians in Van. Nonetheless, you can be sure that not a single drop of Armenian blood will be spilled in Syria.*

A string of events in Aleppo left the Armenians there feeling overwhelmed and subdued. In Aleppo, seven Armenians from Sueda[3] were shot as deserters, one of whom did not die despite having been shot several times. Aleppo's Tashnags[4] were imprisoned and forced to do hard labor. All Armenian officials were dismissed; correspondence in Armenian was forbidden; sending money or anything else to an Armenian's address was forbidden. Travel was absolutely forbidden; doing significant trade was impossible, and contract work was denied to the Armenians. If Turkish officials had to deal with an Armenian in the course of their work, they would postpone the Armenian's issue, saying: *You, dog; you'll have to wait.*

Groups of Armenian deportees from the western *vilayets* (Konia, Gesaria, Izmid, and their environs) were complete (that is to say, the men were with their families), and part of these deportees were in and around Aleppo at the time. But from October 1915, the government began behaving arbitrarily toward these exiles, as well. It often occurred that male members of a family would be out working, and suddenly, the police would come and collect whoever they found on the streets and send them to the train station, to be driven to Resulayn. During these unexpected relocations, the government of course would not consider the fact that part of the family remained in Aleppo, powerless and helpless. Up until that month, the Armenians from the western *vilayets* had remained untainted, but once they had been sent, group by group, to Resulayn, where there was no security of life or honor at all, they too were subjected to the conditions faced by the Armenians from Armenia.

The train stopped in Jarābulus's station, and we saw that a compartment of one of the cars was being rigorously inspected.

Through the windows, we saw men in black with discolored faces, but it was impossible to approach them; they also were careful not to make any sign and attract the attention of the police. We realized that these were the notable Armenian intellectuals[5] deported from Istanbul, who were being taken to face

---

[3] [AM] Suedia, a city in the Adana *vilayet*, in the region of Alexandretta (İskenderun).
[4] [AM] Founded in 1890, the *Hay Heghapokhagan T'ashnagts'utiwn* (Armenian Revolutionary Federation) is a political party that still holds prominence in Armenian life today. At the time, they called for a free Armenia, but not necessarily through independent statehood. Its members had participated in the Ottoman Parliament and were allied for a time with the Young Turks, but were nonetheless targeted during the genocide.
[5] [ZY] These must have been those individuals separated from the group of exiled intellectuals at Ayash and sent to Dikranagerd. These were the following: Khachadur Malumian, Rupen Zartarian,

judgment in Dikranagerd. Did the trial take place? What was the result? We could not ascertain the answers to these questions. We only heard this much from Turks from Dikranagerd: *The important Armenian intellectuals came to Dikranagerd, were condemned, and will be hanged.*

Beyond Arap Punar, they had transported the Armenians by cart; and upon his return, the Turkish coachman praised their admirable and noble conduct and felt sorry for them.

Since they were ill, Zohrab and Vartkes[6] remained in Aleppo's Rod al-Faraj inn for eleven days, then were sent by train to Edessa (Urfa). They had written a letter to Jemal Pasha from Aleppo, whose contents I do not know, and had received the following reply: *I am ready to aid you financially. As much as you would like.*

The Turkish deputy to the Ottoman Parliament from Edessa, a very noble man who was friendly toward Armenians, had greeted the two Armenians in Edessa and even hosted them in his home. He tried very hard to keep the deputies in his home and take full responsibility for them, but the government—especially the Chechen *reisi*[7] Halil *bey*, who had come from Istanbul with Arnaut vagrants to organize the massacres of Armenians in the regions of Dikranagerd, Mardin, and Kharpert—resisted this; and on just the second day, Zohrab and Vartkes were sent by cart to Dikranagerd. But they had barely traveled one hour from Edessa, when Halil *bey*, who was also present, ordered the cart to descend near Karakopru. The two deputies are told to deboard, and Zohrab gets out of the cart. But understanding everything, Vartkes turns to Halil *bey* and says: *I know you have come to kill us. I am sick: kill me in my cart.* But Halil *bey* had already aimed his pistol at Zohrab, and the second shot struck Vartkes. Vartkes' blood painted the cart. Upon his return, the coachman recounted these details, and

---

Dr. Daghavarian, Sarkis Minas, and Jihangulian, Khazhag.
[AM] A reference to the Armenian intellectuals, notables, and political leaders rounded up in Istanbul on April 24, 1915. One group was sent to Ayaş and interned there. On June 2, the six main political leaders, listed by the author in this note, were officially sent to Dikranagerd to face a court-martial but were, in fact, murdered halfway between Edessa and Severeg. Their murders marked the beginning of the liquidation of the Istanbul Armenian elites. For more information, see Kevorkian, *The Armenian Genocide: A Complete History*, New York and London: I.B. Tauris & Co Ltd, 201.

[6] [ZY] Erzrum's Armenian deputies to the Ottoman Parliament in Constantinople; [TN] Krikor Zohrab (also a prominent writer and lawyer) was the deputy from Istanbul; here, the reference is also to Vartkes Serengulian from Erzrum. Although they were not deported on April 24, they were not spared and were ultimately killed in a gorge named Şeytan Deresi two hours from Urfa.

[7] [MA, TMB] From Arabic, meaning "chief" of a group, a clan, or a tribe. It was also used as a military title for naval captains in the Ottoman Empire.

pointing to the spots of blood, said: *This is the blood of your deputy, who Khalil Bey killed with his own hands.*

The coachman's words confirmed the story of an Armenian merchant's wife from Edessa, who had heard it herself from the coachman. The same story with the same details was repeated by many Armenians and Turks in Edessa.

13

The Edessa (Urfa) Resistance. The First Steps of Deportation. The Armenians Are in Revolt. Negotiations. A Turkish Army Besieges the Armenian Quarter. Fifteen Days of Fighting. Edessa Ruined. The Former Situation.

The government had planned the deportation of Edessa, but in order to avoid a general resistance, the Turks turned to various forms of deception. In line with their plans, they removed the city's powerful individuals, one by one, and in advance.

At first, forty notables and the prelate were detained and taken to the local prison, which was the horse stable. The Turks say that they tortured the Armenians considerably. When the Armenians ask to take food to the prelate and the other prisoners, they are forbidden from doing so. On the second day, the prisoners are moved to a different place and disappear.

Then the authorities demanded 100 Armenians from the merchant class. Although thousands of liras were handed over to the officials and soldiers, who gave their word to keep the prisoners in the city, those 100 individuals were also sent away; it is not clear where they were sent, and they also disappeared. Then another 100 followed them.

The Edessa Armenians knew about the situation faced by the Armenians from Armenia; they had seen their pitiable caravans; they had heard of the horrible incidents that had taken place there. And now, they saw the deportation of Edessa beginning in exactly the same manner. They knew that if they submitted, the result would be the abduction of boys and girls; the massacre of men; the violation of women; death and horror; and all those shocking incidents they had already seen with their own eyes.

The Armenian women were furious and obstinate, and they forced their men to no longer submit and allow themselves to be handed over to the government.

At the same time, the city's Turks had sent word to the beautiful Armenian women, saying: *If the Armenians are deported from Edessa, you don't have to worry: you and your children will stay with us. You're ours.*

Before the fighting had even begun, Circassians and Turks would knock on the Armenians' doors and demand money and girls. When refused, they threatened to massacre the Armenians on the day of their deportation. The homes where men were no longer present, as a result of their having already been deported or conscripted, were subjected to nighttime assaults by young local Turks, who would plunder, terrorize, and commit all kinds of evils.

Edessa's Armenian women already had strong organizations, through which they maintained an orphanage, a workshop, a society of the Red Cross, and so on. As a last resort, all the members of those organizations agreed and prepared to poison themselves instead of falling into the enemy's hands.

The government continued to demand men in groups of hundred, but the people resisted; no one turned themselves in. At the women's suggestions, the men no longer went down to the market and instead remained hidden in the Armenian quarter, which was in the upper district; only the women continued working. In order to get ahead of the prospect of violence, the Armenians had paid hundreds of thousands of liras, but the authorities strictly demanded that the men be handed over, especially the eldest of the Yedikardashian brothers. This brother was crippled and wanted, but he nonetheless descended into the city every day wearing different disguises. He would even enter the government buildings and find out the orders and information given about the Armenians.

The government had sent away the Armenians who had come to Edessa from Armenia and had strictly forbidden local Armenians from leaving the city, for any reason.

The government had also sent the Europeans from Syria, who were being held in Edessa as prisoners of war, to a nearby location set aside specifically for them.

All this worried the Armenians, who knew what was being prepared for them. They were hiding in their quarter and did not let any foreigner in, since Turks and Kurds had recently been allowed to enter any Armenian home they wished and to do whatever their diabolical imaginations wanted to them.

In those days, a group of policemen went to search an Armenian home. There was no man in the house, and only a mother and daughter were left. The daughter's beauty enticed the chief officer, who—wanting to satiate his desire after the fruitless search—ordered his policemen to forcibly take the girl to one of the house's rooms, where her brother was secretly hiding. When the officer approaches the Armenian girl, her brother, unable to withstand the danger faced by his sister, jumps out of his hiding spot and shoots the policeman. Panic, cries, and clamor rule in the house; then, the officers flee and frightfully spread the word among the Turkish population, that the Armenians are in revolt.

The government immediately takes advantage of this incident and sounds the alarm among the Turks. The local military authorities telegraph Aleppo: *Quickly send aid. Edessa is in danger: the Armenians are in revolt.* This is why Fakhri Pasha is quickly sent from Aleppo to open an investigation and take any necessary action.

Fahri Pasha was by nature not such a bad man. He was forced to enact the orders he was given, but he preferred to arrange everything as smoothly as possible; and he did not refuse to alleviate the Armenians' situation whenever he had the opportunity. Instead of hanging 300 people in Zeytun, he sent them to Damascus. In Hajin, when the population refused to obey the deportation commands for three days, he tried to convince the Armenians to peacefully leave rather than using violence. When he was informed of the condition of the Armenians in the Nizib khan, he worked to ameliorate their situation.

Arriving in Edessa this time, he opened an investigation and immediately discovered that the news sent to Aleppo was incorrect and that the Armenians were not in a state of revolt. But since the deportation of the Armenians from Edessa had already been decided and its enactment handed over to him, he entered into negotiations with the Armenians and convinced them to submit to the order, promising to provide ease and security.

The Armenians accepted his propositions, but on one condition: that he return the 250 men who had already been arrested and deported. Once they were reunited with their relatives, the Armenians would then hand themselves over and go to the place designated for them by the government. Fahri Pasha would have liked to fulfill the Edessa Armenians' request, but it was impossible, since those men had already been killed.

But the Armenians saw that Fahri Pasha was deceptively delaying their request, saying that they would be reunited with their relatives at a certain place. The Armenians did not want to fall victim to those usual tricks and thus declared, with finality, that they would not be leaving their homes.

In October 1915, based on the information sent by Fahri Pasha, on the orders of Jemal Pasha, as it was supposed, a military force was sent to Edessa from Aleppo. It was comprised of regular soldiers, three cannons, four to five machine guns, several officers, and everything else necessary for an army. The local authorities had already gathered the region's Kurds and armed them along with the local Turks and the Circassians from Bunbuj. The Turks from Birecik and its surrounding areas also went as volunteers to plunder and massacre Edessa's Armenians. Thus, the Armenian quarter was surrounded by tens of thousands.

The Armenians had given their young men as soldiers to the Turkish army, so their young and fighting force was in need. The government had just deported the wealthy and young men and had sent away many others on the pretext that they were artisans. But the women and girls, armed with their valor, joined the few men who made up the seed of the resistance. These women and girls vowed to die fighting instead of passing into the hands of the vile enemy and being subjected to dishonors.

The fighting began. The assault on the Armenian quarter took place from four sides. Rifle smoke hung over the quarter each day from morning to noon. It was undoubtable that there was no hope of salvation for the Armenians, but their spirits were high. They withstood the enemy's barrages with song and joy, responding bravely and leaving many Turkish corpses behind. The Turks from Edessa, who had initially opened fire, had almost entirely fallen. A state of panic and confusion had set in, especially since the regular army had not been successful in taking the Armenian quarter. All the while, Armenian girls would emerge out of unknown corners and throw grenades into the Turkish mob and disappear.

The city's Turks gradually fled, and for a brief time, the Armenians were in control of all Edessa. The crowd of Turks and Kurds surrounding the city grew weaker and more afraid. Many left and, returning to their homes, recounted exaggerated and fantastical tales about the Armenian force. The regular soldiers were forced to make their siege more complete, and another assault took place; this one happened with extreme vehemence. There were Arab soldiers among them, to whom the Armenians called out: *You are our brothers, why are you fighting against us? We will not strike you. Leave here now.*

The battle lasted fifteen days, during which time Edessa's renown, the celebrity of its brave Armenians, and especially the reputation of the Yetikartashians, spread to the surrounding regions. Confounded by this unexpected resistance, the government ordered the authorities on the ground to act with finality. Fahri Pasha wanted to keep the Armenians besieged without destroying the city, and to thus starve them out. But the military council in Aleppo ordered him to use artillery to bring a quick end to the resistance. The artillery thundered from October 16 to October 20, and the Armenian quarter and church were destroyed. They even destroyed buildings far from the Armenian quarter that had not been part of the fighting. But even this ruination did not succeed in subduing the Armenians, who continued desperately resisting. The enemy army was in a state of confusion, because they had not ascertained in advance that the Armenians had prepared underground shelters. These dugouts had existed for a long time. But the Armenians, sensing what was going to befall them, had partly renovated the dugouts and adapted them to their needs, amassing stores of food there. They had complete provisions, a well, shelters for the citizens, and had even secured routes of communication outside the front lines. When the enemy understood the role these dugouts and tunnels played, they aimed their guns at the ground and destroyed the routes. Seeing the Armenians firing at them through the smoke, they charged and broke the resistance with a final assault. The Turkish soldiers rushed upon the Armenian quarter and began mercilessly massacring the homeless population. The young men and girls were still fighting; scattered groups and individual women and men fought until their last breaths; many women had poisoned themselves and were writhing beneath soldiers' legs; confused, the children and elderly wandered in the ruins; while off in the distance, a group of Armenian girls and boys burned Armenian possessions, amassing rugs, furniture, even foodstuffs, and destroying everything, so that nothing would fall into the hands of the enemy.

The Turks finally seized the Armenian quarter and began collecting the children, the elderly, and the fighting men and women they had succeeded in capturing alive. The Turkish soldiers looked with surprise upon the structures of the Armenian dugouts and the corpses of the fallen Armenian girls, whose breasts were adorned with cartridge belts. Almost moved, they said to each other: *Is such a thing really possible?*

The government had seized about 2,000 people, of whom about 200 were men. 60 of these men were hanged in Edessa for authoring the revolt, and the remaining 140 were sent to Aleppo to stand trial. The women[1] and children were deported to Mesopotamia.

The Turks and Kurds who had come from the surrounding areas to plunder the Armenians left empty-handed and terrified, as some Armenians continued to fire their rifles until they were killed.

In 1895, Edessa was subjected to an extremely violent massacre. But in a short amount of time, the Armenians had remedied their losses and regained their former position. Having good relations with the Arabs, they had come to lead villages. They owned almost all the region's agricultural products. Commerce

---

[1] [ZY] A woman from Edessa who witnessed the revolt, and whose story in no way contradicts that of Haig Toroyan, said that women and girls who had fought were also hanged.

and artisanship, which were entirely in the hands of the Armenians, had again flowered.

After the reestablishment of the Ottoman constitution, the carpet workshops were expanded and the carpet trade with America received an impulse. The women's embroidery society also flourished, and a large portion of their products were also exported to America. The Armenians wanted to work with the Kurdish and Turkish landholders to modernize their agricultural practices, and the Armenians undertook the task of introducing new machinery and fortifying irrigation systems. At the demand of the local population, a branch of the Ottoman Bank was opened, along with an agricultural bank, and so on.

Not only did the Armenians' economic life improve but so too did their intellectual life. They had theaters, auditoria, separate men's and women's libraries, as well as unions of young people established with the goal of enlightening the population.

The German railway line could reach a point, which was four hours in distance from Edessa. This circumstance was a great opportunity for improving commerce, which helped the region gradually grow richer. The Germans gave preference to the Armenians. Knowing their diligence and scrupulosity, they entrusted the Armenians with contract work; they chose them as their intermediaries in trade; and they turned to their artisans when they needed them. The Armenians had already achieved the best positions in terms of commerce and agriculture. They had again begun to buy vast fields, vineyards, and orchards and build white stone houses in the European style, inside of which they led wealthy lives.

All of this not only incited the local Turks but also unsettled the government. Knowing very well that the Muslim presence, despite its majority, was incapable of competing with the Armenians, the authorities had here begun, as in other Armenian-inhabited areas, to use government measures, such as economic boycott and other persecutions, to weaken the Armenians' economic and intellectual strength.

This tense and hostile situation already existed by the time the war had broken out.

14

A Wedding Among the Kurds. A Temporary Order Concerning the Property of the Exiled Armenians. The Birecik Armenians Convert to Islam, yet Are Still Deported. The Words of a Turkish Soldier from Marash.

The vast majority of Birecik's residents are Kurds or Turks, with Kurdish and Arab[1] roots. The sheikhs propagandized fervently among these Muslims, telling them to marry Armenian girls and adopt Armenian children. They said that from a religious perspective, these actions were *sevab* (acceptable to God) and that they contributed to the betterment of the Turkish race. This propaganda was so widespread that proposals and letters asking for Armenian girls arrived from all over. Many came in person to take these girls.

Turkish or Kurdish workers, officials, soldiers, or gendarmes in distant places, and who were unable to travel, promised those who would bring them a girl or woman a payment of eight to ten *kese* (every *kese* is 500 *ghurush*), a cow, ten sheep, and so on in accordance with their abilities. As a result of this sentiment toward Armenian girls, there were hardly any left in Birecik—even the ugly ones had been taken away. In many places, taking an Armenian girl was seen as bravery, something worthy of praise.

A wealthy Kurd had succeeded in finding a beautiful Armenian girl for his son, and to celebrate this triumph, he had invited all the region's villagers to their wedding. He organized a mounted procession, seated the Armenian maiden on a horse, and ornamented her with precious silks, diamonds, and ornaments. In front of the girl, Kurdish women in colorful clothes, including the groom's mother and close female relatives, danced and sang in groups, while the groom, himself dressed in opulent garments, raced on horse with other young men

---

[1] [ZY] Those nomadic Arabs and Kurds who settle in cities and villages become Turks or are now known by that name.

were playing with swords. Led by the *davul* and *zurna*,[2] this procession of guests marched through the villages, boasting of the Armenian bride's merits. The feasting and merriment lasted three days.

Around that time, the Turkish newspapers published a provisional law, which was also reprinted in the *Puzantion*[3] daily.

The law was made up of three articles, and its enactment was overseen by a committee established by Talat *bey*.[4]

The law related to the confiscation of the moveable and immoveable properties of the deported Armenians. The committee had the authority to sell the Armenians' property and to pay their creditors. The remainder would be handed back to the owners, if they were present. If they were not, the properties would remain in the hands of the committee.

The committee had already begun its work on the basis of this law. They hastily sold the Armenians' homes, gardens, fields, and so on. Meanwhile, Armenian creditors were not allowed to collect any payment.

Birecik's Armenians were in a critical situation. Not only had they seen and heard about the state of the Armenians deported from other places, and about the horrible aftermaths of those deportations, but at the same time, they were themselves being harassed by local Turks, who were extremely bigoted and who used every available opportunity to threaten the local Armenians. Brutal provocations took place almost daily. For example, a Turk leaves a package at an Armenian's store, saying he'll be back in half an hour to collect it. He then goes straightaway to inform the government that there is a gun and ammunition at this or that Armenian store. The police immediately arrive, search the store, and finding the package that the Turkish neighbor had left—and therein a gun and some cartridges. As a result, they take the shopkeeper into their custody. The Armenian gives his word and begs for mercy, but these pleas are useless.

These types of incidents, which put these people in a constant state of threat, have made the Birecik Armenians desperate. As a means to save themselves, they decided to convert to the Turks' religion. A hundred families, the entirety of Birecik's Armenian population, accepted Islam and conducted all the external formalities of conversion. They even demolished the Armenian church's belfry. They conducted the funeral procession of an Armenian woman, who had died

---

[2] [AM] The *davul* is a traditional drum, while the *zurna* is a wind instrument. Both are used in the folk music of the various peoples of Anatolia.

[3] [AM] An Armenian-language daily newspaper published in Istanbul (1896–1918).

[4] [AM] Reference to Mehmed Talat Pasha (1874–1921), a member of the Young Turk movement and leader of the triumvirate ruling the Ottoman Empire from 1913 to 1918 (along with Enver and Jemal Pasha), he was the architect of the Armenian genocide.

during that time, in accordance with Islamic practices and buried her in the Turkish cemetery. Only the old priest had not renounced his faith and remained holed up in the church, praying incessantly.

The Turkish population, and even the government, accepted this conversion with great respect. They requested that the Sheikh al-Islam in Istanbul authenticate these conversions with a decree, which he did. The government then began handing out new identification papers to the Islamized Armenians. As such, relations between the Turks and Armenians ameliorated. The Turks had begun to see these Islamized Armenians as friends—that is, until the revolt in Edessa and the Armenian neighborhood, which has positioned on high ground, raised suspicions among government circles, especially in the mind of Fahri Pasha.

On November 12, notwithstanding the Turkish population and the sheikhs' appeals, all the Birecik Armenians were deported to Mesopotamia.

A Turkish soldier from one of Marash's villages, hearing of the deportations of Armenians from his village, complained about the government:

> We lived with our Armenian neighbors like brothers, and they satisfied all our needs without complaint. Whenever I needed to go into the city on business, they always furnished me with a horse or donkey without refusing. I would sometimes even need to keep the animal for days. Whenever I bought something from their stores, they wouldn't ask me for the money straight away, but would tell me not to worry, that I could pay them later. I would sometimes pay after five or six months. My children would play with theirs, learning their tales and songs. Our children loved the Armenians so much that they wouldn't leave their Armenian houses until evening. When I joined the army, my neighbors[5] took care of all the expenses of my household. When my relative, Ali, expressed to me that my home was not lacking thanks to how my Armenian neighbor cared for it, my heart was at peace. But now, hearing that my good neighbors have been deported, I'm losing my mind. I don't understand why they would commit such evil against such good people. How about my agony... what will become of my household?

---

[5] [MA, TMB] That is, Armenian neighbors.

15

The Turks' Suspicious Attitude Toward Me and the Other Local Armenians. Jarābulus's the German Hospital at Jarābulus. Captain Otto Oehlmann, a German Officer. My Departure.

The Edessa resistance had provoked the hatred of both the military officials and the Circassians toward the Armenians—and especially toward me, since I had always endeavored to help the Armenians passing through Jarābulus and there had often been complaints about me to the government. They considered the time ripe to inflict damages onto the Armenians and to take revenge on me. I had already long felt that my situation was not secure. And so, a Turkish writer friend of mine, who was a young free-thinking anti-Ittihadist, told me that the Circassian Mustafa was preparing a plot against me and that it was imperative that I leave Jarābulus.

German soldiers were always traveling down the Euphrates by boat, on the way toward Baghdad. This gave me the idea that I could leave Jarābulus by securing a position with any one of these soldiers. To that end, I appealed to an Armenian doctor I knew, who was the head doctor at the local German hospital and whose wife was German. At that point, a German captain named Otto Oehlmann, whose gentle character had attracted the attention of the head doctor, lay in the hospital. The doctor offered to make an introduction. Meanwhile, the hospital accountant also promised to intercede on my behalf. They introduced me to Mr. Otto Oehlmann, a thirty- to thirty-five-year-old man who was considerably tall and had a handsome face. His duty was to transport guns to Persia, which he would do by traveling down the Euphrates to Baghdad and on from there to the border. I know all the local languages and dialects that are spoken along the route (Arabic, Kurdish, Turkish, etc.), and so, we agreed that I would accompany him as his translator. As soon as we met, he asked me: *Are you Armenian?* When I responded in the affirmative, he accepted me gladly. We spoke for about half an hour and agreed that we would depart the following morning, on November 12, 1915. My departure from Jarābulus was difficult, especially since it was impossible for me to pretend I was not Armenian, something we planned to do after setting off. But Otto Oehlmann took great pains to ensure that the gendarmes would not prevent me from boarding the boat. We had ten boats in our care, which were loaded with military supplies, and we were accompanied by ten gendarmes who did not know me. The German officer suggested that I hide the fact that I was Armenian from the beginning, and so, I pretended to be a Syrian Catholic Arab man called Yusuf.

Our boat had a small wooden room, in which we both slept and ate. We had very good provisions for the journey, even drinks. Even from the beginning, I was surprised by the brotherly trust the German officer placed in me. He asked that we take our midday and evening meals together. He told me about his previous life in Tabriz, where he had a wife and newborn son. He spoke of them longingly, as he was impatient to reach Persia, where he would finally take his leave and rejoin them. He said that in Tabriz, he could only have pleasant friendships with Armenians. He had relationships with local Armenian merchants, had attended their evening parties, and had many opportunities to interact with the Armenian community as vice-consul. And every time he had traveled on business, he met Armenians in Turkey and Russia, of whom he spoke only with praise—especially the Armenians of Istanbul, whose intellectual and economic life had left him stunned.

When I asked him why he wanted his translator to be Armenian, he replied: *I am an experienced man, and I am familiar with the quality of work done by my Armenian employees, and their trustworthiness. But as for you in particular, when the time comes, I will show you why I took an Armenian translator.*

Once, I was complaining about my material losses, expressing that everything had been ruined as a result of these past incidents, and I also spoke of the horrific torments borne by the Armenians. The German officer explained honestly that all of this caused him great pain. After speaking with disgust about the impotence and brutality of the Turkish government, he additionally found fault with the Armenians, who he claimed were disorganized and unprepared in their moment of crisis.

> We thought highly of the Armenians, he said. We knew how much you toiled, how your commercial life was flourishing, and we even knew as much as the number of your schools. You had partisan organizations: why did you have to be slaughtered this way, like sheep? Your resistance would not have surprised us, but this situation is inexplicable.

He provided the Edessa resistance as an example:

> If the Armenians had been as organized as we had thought they were, and if Armenians everywhere had raised a united cry, their voice would not have remained unheard.

He marveled at the Germans' military force and the technological means they possessed, but he also spoke respectfully about the English and French. He especially liked the Russian Cossacks, with whom he had traveled frequently. He hated war and mocked the Turks' simple-mindedness and ignorance, without going into details. He said that all the German officers officially conducted themselves with respect toward the Turks, but that when they were alone, the Turks became an inexhaustible object of ridicule and sarcasm. He had been a secretary at the German military office in Istanbul and had witnessed with his own eyes how unprepared the Turkish military was. Even high-ranking *pashas* spoke haphazardly and were often confounded. Without German aid, the Turks would have been subjected to a quick and ridiculous defeat.

Conversing like this as we traveled down the Euphrates, we reached Meskene in three days (November 15).

16

Meskene. The Teacher. Toward Raqqa.[1]

At Meskene, there are two vast sandy fields on both sides of the Euphrates. On the right bank, there is a large *khan* and a small telegraph office, where the local military *kaymakam* lives.

My officer said: *Let's go see the Armenians.* We descended onto the right bank together, and after advancing for ten minutes, guided by a gendarme, we reached a place where about 1,500 Armenians were strewn about the field, having only ten to eleven umbrella-like tents as shelter. These were Armenians from Mersin, Kharpert, Izmid, and Adana. The men were small in number and only from Cilicia or the western provinces. The ill were fallen all about, writhing in the sand, sighing, and they begged for compassion whenever they saw someone pass. A woman sat on the road, rocking her dying child in her lap. When she saw us approaching, she fell to her knees and looked at us imploringly. My officer immediately turned around, and said: *Hurry back.* He shut his eyes and hastily moved away. When I approached him, he said: *Let's go, we have quinine and medicine for diarrhea. I'll give them to you, and you can distribute them, because that child has a severe fever.*

Having received the medicine, I returned to the group of deportees. Suspecting that my aunt's daughter Anna could be among them, I searched among the groups, accompanied by a gendarme. Suddenly, I saw a girl of about twenty-five with a pretty face and relatively clean clothes. She was wandering about the field, talking to the exiles and consoling them. Everyone listened to her with respect. Pointing to this girl, the gendarme suggested I take her with me for my pleasure, and he took me to her to this end. I approached the girl, and restraining the gendarme from saying anything inappropriate, I began speaking with her in Turkish.

Where are you from? I asked.

---

[1] [MA, TMB] Raqqa or Ar Raqqah is a city in Syria on the left bank of the Euphrates River, east of Aleppo.

Izmid (Nicomedia).
How are you getting by?
Miserably, as you can see; sick and hungry . . .
What are you doing, walking like this among the groups?
I find consolation in encouraging and consoling the people.

When I found out that she knew French, we began speaking in that language. She did not complain about their misery nor about the government's conduct; she only fearfully pointed out the lack of bread and medicine.

Our conversation had lasted quite a long time until I noticed that her face had begun to lose color. She started trembling and then fainted. Voices cried out from all around us: *Even our teacher has fallen from hunger.*

The gendarme wanted to take the unconscious girl away, but I threatened him, using the name of my German officer. Growing scared, he was forced to move away.

I returned to our boat to get more medicine and money. Then, I went back to the Armenians. The teacher was awake but still ill. I distributed the bread and medicine to those exiled people. Seeing that I was distributing bread, the people rushed upon me from everywhere, and I was hardly able to free myself. They all cried: *Effendi, bread! Effendi, medicine! . . .*

Arab women had come from distant places and were selling thin branches for burning, which hardly weighed one *oka*,[2] at 20 *paras*. The midday heat was bearable, but the nighttime cold, especially the dew, was deadly. Human excrement lay in piles around the Armenians, and meanwhile the miserable population was trying to get all kinds of dirt out of themselves.

At that time, new refugees were arriving from Aleppo. The arrivals could not even sit. They would throw themselves to the ground and immediately lay down. In a mad state, they seemed to have lost all their senses. And the Armenians already there showed no interest in these newcomers, overcome as they were with their own suffering. Rows of people, fallen some were crying, some were moaning, and no one to ask them about their pain; they did not even speak with one another. When I would ask: *Is there anyone from Kharpert here?* They would simply point. I sometimes spoke for a long time without receiving any reply: their gazes fixed on my eyes or some random point; they would remain motionless and would not want to utter a single syllable.

---

[2] [MA, TMB] The *oka, oke,* or *okka* was an Ottoman measure of mass which equaled to 400 Ottoman *drams*. In the late empire, it was standardized as 1.2829 kilograms.

When I returned to the boat, I saw that the local Turkish officer had come to greet the German. When I asked the officer why he was not providing bread for the Armenians, he said: *I don't have enough bread for my soldiers, how am I supposed to feed the Armenians? Although, I regard their situation as very sad, and I've even telegraphed about it. But what can I do?*

Darkness descended on my country. The German officer, affected by what he had seen during the day, was sorrowful. He neither smoked nor drank, although he was accustomed to at that time of day. Pensive and cheerless, he sat alone; it was as if he was cautious even to speak with me.

Our gendarmes returned again and secretly suggested that I go and enjoy the Armenian women. *God has made them for us, they said, for us to meet them here.*

The German officer had strictly forbidden the gendarmes from leaving their boats, but they left at night and returned very late, almost at sunrise.

In the morning, we left Meskene for Raqqa, and a short time later, we saw a corpse floating on the river. We gradually approached it and began to discern her clothing and face. The gendarmes and I screamed: *It's the teacher from yesterday! The teacher!*

At that point, the gendarmes recounted their exploits from the previous night:

> How foolish that you didn't come with us. We went with the local corporal to the Armenians, took this girl to the corporal's room, and enjoyed her until morning. But you should have seen how feisty she was: she tried to persuade us, like a lawyer. She answered us so daringly and said things that left us stunned. But finally, she gave up, became angry, and started yelling, You're worse than wild beasts.

The gendarmes had tortured her terribly, and fleeing their grasp for a moment, she had thrown herself into the river.

The teacher's corpse flowed calmly down the river, and her untied hair undulated with the small waves. Her face was hidden beneath a thin layer of water.

Early the next morning, we saw men and women who had descended to the left bank of the river. Some wore white pajamas; many were dressed in European fashions, even the women. They washed with soap and even had pretty facecloths. Our boats passed very close to them, and we saw their faces. Each of them threw a reproachful glance at us as they moved away. The German officer said: *Look, it's as if they're cursing us.*

Our boats advanced, and we saw, behind a small hill, the homes of those deportees. They had constructed low and relatively clean adobes. There were also a few huts made of reed, in front of which a great number of similarly dressed deportees were gathered. We were not able to find out where those Armenians were from.

Since our next stop was far away, we disembarked when it became night. We would sometimes go with our gendarmes to the Arab tents in the desert, which were a fifteen-minute walk from the riverbank. On one such evening, we arrived at the Arab tents and heard that there were Armenians in one of them. I immediately wanted to know which tent they were in, but the gendarmes had already gone and searched it, and returning, they told me: *Don't go there. There's nothing: no girls or young women.*

The tent was woven from animal hair and divided into three sections, one of which held the Arabs' cattle and sheep. In the second section, which was hardly 4 square meters, forty to fifty old men and women were crowded together. When I entered the tent, they all stood up at once to greet me; they thought me a government official. Their situation was horrible; naturally, there was no room to lie down, and they slept seated. Not only young children but also adolescents slept in their mothers' laps. Nonetheless, when I asked after their condition, they became fearful, and feigning satisfaction, they began praying with trembling voices for the sultan's longevity. Their horrible spiritual situation had a terrible effect on me. I wanted to leave immediately, but my accompanying gendarme, wanting to honor me, demanded the Arab to provide me with a mule. The Arab pointed to the only remaining mule, a very gaunt mule, that belonged to the Armenians and was tied up in front of the tent. When the gendarme approached the mule, the Armenians' faces altered completely. At that point, deeply agitated, I said loudly: *I don't want it. Leave the mule, I'll walk back.*

But now, afraid of my refusal, the Armenians implored me, saying: *Mount it and go! Let it be helal for you.*

They did not know that it would be worse for them, if I were to take the mule. Their confusion, their fear had affected me greatly. I also did not know what I could do to put them at ease. I was forced to take the mule, and an Armenian boy accompanied me to bring it back. As we rode, I revealed to him that I was a Christian so I could make him feel more secure. At that point, he told me that they were from around Marash, and he recounted with sorrow the suffering they had endured. Hungry and thirsty, they were forced to move every day. The Arabs only gave them a piece of black bread. The mule was his, and the poor beast carried the entire group's loads during their aimless wanderings. Whenever they would stop, the mule was given no time to rest: all who passed—soldiers, officers, and gendarmes—would take the mule by force and use it to pull unbearable loads. When the mule was unable to do so, the boy was forced to whip it or carry some of the load himself. This mule, which should have eased the deportees' situation, had become their scourge, and in this way, the mule had shared in its owners' fate.

> The mule already doesn't have anything to eat," said the boy. "Like us, it's living off dried grass from wherever it can find it."

Our accompanying gendarmes had brought sacks of flour with them to sell at high prices to the deported Armenians.

One night, as the gendarmes were busy selling flour, groups of Armenians rushed on us from every corner. Those who had money gave it; most paid with all sorts of objects. Some even wanted to sell their children or their honor, but the gendarmes and boatmen refused; they demanded either money or possessions instead.

The Armenians hastily lit fires here and there. Those who had purchased flour (who were considered the fortunate and wealthy ones) went aside and began baking bread. They quickly formed dough, kneaded it into a circle without salt or leaven; then, they threw the circle into the fire. They would stack slips of straw around the dough, lighting it and waiting impatiently. But the dough was not yet cooked when they began plucking off pieces and ravishing the dough, burning their fingers in the meantime. Those who were unable to buy flour were faintly lying all over the floors. From every corner, weak groans and moans were being heard. The children of these unfortunate ones lingered around the fires and begged for bread, sometimes even from their own aunts, but in their extreme and superhuman misery, the deportees had become uncompassionate and inflexible and did not even answer these starving children.

My focus turned to a group of children crowded around a sack of flour, who were licking their fingers to collect and eat the flour that had fallen on the ground.

17

Raqqa. The Armenian Cemetery. The Sight of the People Gone Mad in the Field. The State of the Exiles on the Left Bank in Raqqa. The Burial of a Girl.

Sandy fields spread out on both sides of the river. In the middle of the river, there was a small island, on which we could see some greenery. On the right bank was the city of Raqqa, with 600 to 700 homes, inhabited entirely by Arabs. The homes were made of adobe, and the city had a small market. At 11 o'clock (Turkish time),[1] we arrived at Raqqa, and on the left bank of the Euphrates, we saw a multitude of about 5,000 Armenians from Armenia, Cilicia, and Anatolia (the western provinces). Accompanied by a gendarme, a few young men crossed to the right bank to buy bread and flour. Since night had fallen early, I was unable to go to the city. So, still on the boat, I began looking around me. A few Armenians wandered on the riverbank. I saw that our gendarmes had forcibly loaded the Armenians with the flour they had brought and were taking the flour to the city to be sold. The Armenians on the left bank of the river presented a strange picture. It was as if a fair were taking place there; in the darkness, the groups were completely illuminated by the fires they had lit.

It was past midnight when we awoke to a horrible clamor. The heartrending sounds of women and children, the jackals' howls, and the cries of nighttime thieves coming away with girls or property melded together. The fires had been put out, and we could not see a thing; but the clamor of children sobbing from the night cold, which dominated all the other sounds, made us tremble with anger. A moment later, we found out what happened. The gendarmes had decided at that point to put the exiled people back on the road. One group

---

[1] [MA, TMB] *alla turca time*, also known as *ezani times* or *gurûbî* (sunset time) was a time system used in the Ottoman Empire which was divided between sunrise and sunset, where the sun always set at the zero hour and rose on the twelfth hour. The system was important for prayer times, which were based on the sun's position in the sky.

asleep, one group shivering in the cold, one group huddled together; stupefied, terrified, half-asleep, the exiles were forced to walk in the dark, to be driven into the depths of Mesopotamia.

When dawn broke, there was nobody left on the left bank, and all we saw were the ashes from the extinguished fires scattering in the wind.

The sun rose, and I prepared to depart with one of our gendarmes for the city of Raqqa, which was ten to fifteen minutes away from the riverbank. The German officer had an extremely sad disposition. The sounds from that night had affected him, especially because of the things he had seen on our journey; he was in a dark and sorrowful place. He did not even want to come out into the open air. He sat holed up in his room, astonished that even I could bear to look at the state of my fellow Armenians.

We were advancing through the sandy field, when the gendarme said:

Don't go that way, come this way.

I looked in that forbidden direction, and at first glance, I saw nothing. Then I looked more carefully. The vast sandy field was a billow of countless dunes. This was nothing out of the ordinary. The desert wind sometimes agitates the sand like the sea and forms symmetrical mounds similar to waves. I asked the gendarme:

Why? What's over there?

How is it you can't see? The legs, the skulls of the geavurs are still visible.

It was as if my eyes had finally opened, and I immediately saw everything.
Not hundreds, but thousands of human remains were scattered in the sand.

These had not been buried. Rather, it was clear that they were left behind where they had fallen; and without even assembling the corpses, someone had simply covered them with sand. Here and there, the dogs and hyenas had dug through the sand and pulled out someone's limbs, someone's skull. Despite the gendarme's warning, I went toward that vast cemetery, but it gradually became more and more difficult to advance through it. The skeletons increased in number, and I was afraid that I would press on a corpse with every step, or that my foot would touch a human bone while thrusting deep into a mound of sand. I said to the gendarme:

Is it possible that there are this many dead?

Yes, yes! he replied, laughing. These ones didn't die naturally, and they weren't killed either. These are the first exiles from this summer, who died of thirst. With the gendarmes holding the bank of the Euphrates on horseback, with their bayonets, who from that human flock marching thirty paces away would dare cross the chain to drink water?

When we left this field of corpses, I encountered a local Arab, with whom I spoke at length about the Armenian deportees. He pitied the Armenians; at the same time he also complained that they had become the masters of the market. He explained that, compared to the first days of deportation, the situation of the Armenians had been ameliorated, by then. The story of those dead was horrific and unbelievable. This exhausted multitude of thousands of Armenian deportees, no one knew where from, had been delivered by circuitous routes to this field. They were starving and parched beneath the desert's scorching midday sun; they had been plundered and were naked or half-naked at best. And after all that, they had been forbidden, at gunpoint, from approaching the Euphrates to satiate their thirst. This group of people, who had gone mad from thirst, entirely fell and died in the course of a few days—even as they heard the river flowing only thirty paces away.

The sight of these thousands of corpses and their terrible stench, which the wind carried through the desert to distant oases, affected the local population, engendering unrest among the local Arabs with its sight of such useless cruelty. The government was forced to at least cover the fallen corpses; so it assembled a few Arab soldiers to complete this task. The soldiers, not wanting to stay for long in that rotten place, hastily used their shovels to cover the sand over the dead.

In the open sandy fields on both sides of the road, we saw few men and women wandering aimlessly; this attracted my attention. A man came and went, moving his arms. He stopped at times; it was as if he was fighting someone with his fists. Someone else sat on the ground, his head in his hands, staring at the sand. A distance over, another person drew some kind of lines in the sand, or was doing calculations. Each person thus consumed by their own imaginary tasks, some feverishly fighting with one another, these mad Armenians measured out the entirety of the field without crossing its boundaries. I asked the Arab:

Who are these people? Why are they acting like this?

He answered:

> These people were wealthy where they came from. They came here and lost their minds. The number of these fools increases every day; there weren't as many yesterday.

In the distance, rows of women, girls, and boys were getting water from the river, with pails. Some did their laundry, and many women and girls sat and cried on the riverbank.

When I returned to the boats in the evening, the German soldier I was with explained that an elderly man and woman dressed in black *shalwars*,[2] who were most likely from Konya, had come and sat on the riverbank. They spoke and cried for an hour, then returned to their group.

The path on which we walked was the most solid section, but the inconstant sand still made our walk difficult; our legs still sank into the sand. Meanwhile, in the field wherefrom the Armenians came and went, the sand shifted so much that those exiled people sometimes sank all the way to their knees.

A girl in rags carrying a heavy pail in one hand and a child in the other, came to walk on our road; the ground was hard there. An Armenian boy from Mersin, pointed us out and yelled after her:

> Don't you see these dogs? Why are you on the road? They'll take you, just like they took Asdghig yesterday.

We finally arrived at the city. The market was made up of about a hundred stores, half of which were occupied by Armenians from Cilicia and Anatolia. The Armenians had established a few bakeries, and the owners had received commissions to supply the army with bread. There were Armenian cooks, butcher and kebab shops, and others selling vegetables and other food. There were cobblers, tin-platers, sheet metal workers, coffee merchants, and coppersmiths. There also appeared to be women and children who were traveling vendors and who sold meals and sweets from their different areas, and the Arab population would buy these with great pleasure. Taking advantage of the fact that I was alone, I entered an Armenian grocer's shop. When I revealed to him that I was Christian, the grocer began to complain and lament.

The government had told them that they would live in this country from then on, and that the situation would be reexamined after the war. Whoever had land, an orchard, in their native country would be given land of the same size in Mesopotamia, or they were told the land and orchards would be sold and the money brought here to the owner.

The grocer was from Cilicia. Expressing longing for his homeland, he cried, sobbed with his whole heart.

---

[2] [MA, TMB] Loose fitting trousers commonly worn across the SWANA regions and Asia.

He also complained to me, saying:

Don't consider this state we're in now. All of these goods we got through loans from the Arabs, and we'll hardly be able to save our families from hunger and death with them. But things won't stay like this for long. Today or tomorrow, the government will send us somewhere else

These were all Armenian shops, he said. They were in trade. The government sent these people to unknown places.

When I returned, it was midday, and there was no one left in the field besides the madmen, who feverishly continued occupying themselves with their imaginary tasks. Suddenly, we saw two women carrying another woman's corpse on a piece of wood. They were taking her to the field of the dead, which the government had called "the Armenian cemetery." But on the road, a man pulled at the woman walking from the front, who was still young. The corpse rolled onto the ground, while the man dragged the girl away.

The stops for the Armenian exiles brought from Aleppo were: Meskene, Raqqa, Deir ez-Zor, and so on. The surviving deported Armenians sometimes stay in these places for one month, sometimes longer. At times, they are immediately sent to the depths of Mesopotamia without a chance to rest. Everything hangs on the whims of the gendarmes leading them. New groups constantly arrive, and the previous ones are sent away. Those who open stores, rent homes, or settle down in any other way are from older groups. If the Armenian families stay somewhat long in any of these places, they assemble and immediately establish a life for themselves. Whether beneath tents or in homes, they have brought life and energy to whatever place they have passed through, even during those short stays. The Arab population helped them in every way, but unfortunately, the Armenians never settled permanently in one place.

An order would arrive, or the gendarmes that were moving a group of Armenians would pass a judgment on them; leaving everything behind, the Armenians would be obliged to take to the road toward unfamiliar and distant places.

18

Toward Deir ez-Zor.[1] Marash's Armenian Villagers. The Image of the Population on the Banks of the Euphrates. A Second Meeting with a Group of Armenian Exiles.

We departed from Raqqa on November 19. On the second day, the boatmen stopped on the left bank to buy wood from the deported Armenians. Armenian villagers from the environs of Marash were settled here, and having an aptitude for construction, they had succeeded in bringing life to the desert. They had built about seventy homes on the side of a hill, which were covered by sand tile roofs. In the middle of these homes was a khan piled with high-quality charcoal and bundles of pre-cut wood. Some people had mules, with which they brought goods from the surrounding villages or cities. Here and there, there were piles of melons, watermelons, dates, and so on, and they had formed a sort of bazaar, where even the traveling Arabs went to buy goods. I circulated around the homes quite a bit, and looking through the open doors, I saw that everything was arranged neatly. They had covered the floors of their homes with mats made of small pieces of straw and other threads.

There were, moreover, Armenians fishing on the bank of the Euphrates. Our boatmen, who were Turks, spoke jealously about the Armenians, saying:

The geavurs got rich off the wood from that forest.

---

[1] [MA, TMB] Dier ez-Zor (also Dayru z-Zawr or Dayru z-Zūr) is located in present-day eastern Syria. It lies on the south bank of the Euphrates River. During the Armenian Genocide, Armenians were forcibly deported on death marches in two directions: toward Damascus or along the Euphrates toward the Deir ez-Zor concentration camps in the heart of the Syrian desert. Thousands of Armenians died on these death marches while they were forced to walk through the desert without food or water. The place is symbolic for Armenians as it represents the epicenter of death and systematic killing of the Armenian people. The Armenian Genocide Martyrs' Memorial Church, dedicated to the victims of the Armenian Genocide, was destroyed on September 21, 2014.

There was a military headquarter on the right bank, to which the commander invited me and the German officer. There were about 200 deported Armenian families around that base, who were villagers from Cilicia. They all lived in reed huts they had constructed themselves.

We entered the vast room of their headquarters, where we were welcomed with great respect. There we heard that the majority of functionaries, secretaries, and servants were Armenian. The *mudir*[2] recounted with surprise and praise how the Armenians succeeded, through hard work and ingenuity, in securing the lives of 200 families in this great desert.

I visited the reed huts. Everyone was occupied by diligent labor: a young man chopped wood and piled it up; a woman laid out washed wheat under the sun; another woman took a gendarme's measurements to sew his shirt; even the children were busy working.

When the German officer sought to buy milk, an Armenian adolescent said:

I know where there's milk. What will you give me to show you?

His mother was angry at him for this behavior, but still, he energetically led us to an Arab's home, from whom he received a glass of milk as payment; the German officer I was traveling with also paid him abundantly.

The Armenians settled here were sufficiently healthy, appeared well, were neatly dressed, and it seemed they had not been previously subjected to plunder.

In general, the Armenians from Cilicia were already in a disproportionately good state, especially since the men had remained with their families. It appeared from their living conditions that they enjoyed at least a certain degree of protection under the law.

Our boats set off, and we advanced, watching the uniform flat expanses on both sides of the river. After traveling for a few hours, we saw a group of women on the left bank, a crone with a monstrous face, and a boy like a gypsy—all of them scorched by the sun and their misery, and all with completely deformed faces. They sat entirely naked on the riverbank and washed each other. Despite the fact that the Arab tents, in front of which the Arabs lay, were only a few paces away, and despite the fact that our row of boats were passing very close to them, these Armenians did nothing to cover their naked bodies. Indifferent to our presence, they continued what they were doing and sometimes even rubbed sand on their limbs.

---

[2] [MA, TMB] Armenian transliteration of Ottoman Turkish *mudir* (modern Turkish *müdür*), which means a local "director," "administrator," or "supervisor."

There appeared other groups in the distance: there were groups that were moving, groups that were seated; but always, in whichever direction you looked, groups of abandoned Armenians were present—as far as the eye could see.

Once, we stopped on the riverbank during the day and spent the night there. The next morning, we saw the corporal I had met a month prior in Jarābulus with his group of deportees.

The remainder of those exiles were there, and they had changed drastically in that month. They were staying there on the bank of the Euphrates, miserable and abandoned. They no longer wore their colorful clothing. There were no girls, not even groups of young boys; there remained only bewildered old women, who watched the course of the Euphrates. The presence of our ten boats, our comings and goings, our camera: none of this interested them. It was as if this were all a momentary shade passing before their fixed eyes. Life here had ceased: there was no energy, no noise; there was neither moaning, nor crying. Only a deathly silence that prevailed over everyone. With their knotted hair, naked feet, tattered clothes, blackened faces, overgrown nails, and horrible hollow eyes, they frightened even the gendarmes. No one dared to approach or speak with these ghosts.

The corporal's aide explained how they had reached this state.

> On the day they left a place near Samsat, their exact number was 541. They were in good health, had fine clothing, as well as money and other finery. All of this was taken by the corporal during the journey. When these exiled people became deprived of their material resources, many died from thirst, hunger, exhaustion, and the heat. Still, the group bore this torture and grief bravely; however, when they arrived in Raqqa and were about to leave there, their sorrow reached a maddening level.
>
> Why? What happened in Raqqa?
>
> On the kaymakam's orders, they separated the women into two groups—the older women and elderly to one side, and the boys and young girls to the other. The latter stayed in Raqqa, while the ones you see before you were brought here. We carried out that separation at night, in the dark. I cannot forget that hour. The corporal was yelling out orders while we used force to separate mother from child, sister from sister—while they all clung to each other, not wanting to be separated. But what was even worse: they separated newborns from their mothers, who then fainted and fell.
>
> We were completely spent that day. They resisted us intensely: they didn't fear our threats, or the state of terror we had created, not even the lashes of our whips. A few of them died and stayed there. Meanwhile, the number of people losing their minds grew little-by-little, and a few of them threw themselves into the river every week.

When darkness enveloped the earth, I left my boat. A strange terror took its grip over me. I imagined the earth with its vast, sandy terrain where darkness reigned; in that black silence, I envisioned what I had seen that morning—the group of exiled Armenians, along with countless other similar groups. These people, who remained, were painfully striving to breathe life back into the vigor and prosperity of their cities and towns.

The wind had ceased. The Euphrates moved without a whisper; its white surface being sketched in that all-expansive darkness. Everyone was asleep, and this was a good opportunity to go and speak with the unfortunate Armenians. I walked, sinking into the sand, but the monstrous images from that day suddenly came back to me: those terrifying ghosts; and trembling, I immediately turned around and got back into my boat.

19

Deir ez-Zor. Meeting with the Colonel. The Market. A Girl from Mezere. Before the Pharmacy.

On November 24, we arrived at Deir ez-Zor, where the river splits into two branches that wrap around a large island, connected by a bridge, on the right bank, to a city. There are about 45,000 Arab residents. There are fifteen Armenian homes and an Armenian chapel. More than 10,000 Armenians, deported from all the various Armenian-inhabited regions, can be found in Deir ez-Zor.

These deportees are settled in the following manner: nearly all the Armenians from Cilicia were in earthen houses, shops, and caravanserais; the villagers from Cilicia and one portion of the Armenians from Armenia reside in black tents outside the city; and the remainder are in the open air on the riverbank, in gardens, scattered here and there.

Before even reaching the city, about an hour out, there are already groves, gardens, and water mills. A group of women in one of the gardens were seated on the riverbank. Seeing my European clothing, one of them yelled:

Ghurban ĕllam![1] Are you Armenian? What news from our city?

Our boat floated slowly right by the bank. When we approached the women, I asked in Turkish,

Where are you from?

Another woman, turning to the other woman—the one who called out to me earlier—said:

Didn't I tell you: their faces didn't look Armenian?

---

[1] [MA, TMB] Armenian adaptation of the Turkish expression "*Kurban olayım*," meaning "I'll be a sacrifice for you." The expression is commonly used to show love and care in both the Armenian and Turkish languages.

Nonetheless, they replied:

> We are from Kharpert.

We entered the city and went straight to the local military *kaymakam*, a colonel, who was meant to help us with our important business. Captain Otto Oehlmann asked for information on the state of the deported Armenians here. The colonel replied:

> When you go to the market, you'll see that the Armenians are in a good state. At present, there are more than 10,000 Armenians here, and there are still more on their way. They are diligent, inventive, and hard-working. I hope that our city will soon become beautiful and prosperous like Aleppo and Damascus.

We moved on to the marketplace, which was vast. Armenians were everywhere, dressed in all sorts of attire, including children; all of them were all engaged in commerce. Some were artisans working in shops; some were peddlers loaded with different kinds of goods; and some even had opened wholesale trading establishments. Armenian bakers had prepared beautiful pastries, which the locals bought with hearty appetites. They had built ten bakeries; there were tailors, cobblers, hair-dressers, sheet metal workers, tin-platers, weavers, and so on. Armenian children sold various small European goods, cigar papers, matches, thread, and so forth; they also sold different types of food and sweets.

The fishermen sold fish, and some Armenians sold charcoal from different places.

I met a priest and a teacher from Aintab, who were doing different kinds of work. I met many of my acquaintances, with whom I conversed secretly. They were discontent in many ways; at the same time they felt resigned to their situation; they were at least free from massacres and other horrors. These Armenians were from Cilicia, mostly from Aintab.

Tens of Armenian women from Aintab were seated on the riverbank doing laundry. The German officer I was traveling with suggested that one of them clean our dirty linens. Although the amount of work we had for her was very little, and although our clothing was not washed very well, the German / Oehlmann nonetheless paid the woman 40 *ghurush*. Turning to her friend, she said with praise: *And this is a man of manners*.

We called over an Armenian barber, whom the German officer I was with similarly paid substantially. In general, my officer / he was very affected, and it was as if these small, good deeds relieved him for a period. He no longer spoke with me about his impressions, but his face was contracted with unease; he often sighed.

We went to the baths. Taking advantage of my solitude, I sang an Armenian song of exile. One of the workers came to me, terrified, and said:

Quiet! Your songs are going to get us killed.

He thought I was an Armenian from his village, but when he saw that I was a foreigner and especially that I was with a German officer, he sat next to me; he, too, began crying his pain with *menis*.

At one place where we stopped our boats, there was a narrow passage and a few adobe structures, in which Armenian deportees lived. While I was passing, they asked me:

Agha, where are you from?

I discovered that they were from around Arapgir, and when they found out that I too was Armenian, they called me inside. Forty to fifty women were gathered around me; all of them were knitting socks. They closed the doors and began to speak.

I asked if they had received any word about my cousin, my aunt's daughter; they knew nothing. They all asked anxiously:

Do you have any news about our men? What happened to them? Where are they? They took them, saying they were going to work on the roads, and they brought us here. What a miracle! How did you get away? This means our men can also escape, like you!

I said a few comforting words. Tears fell from everyone's eyes. In the corner, there was a young woman of medium height; she had very dark hair and eyebrows, and red cheeks. She wore colorful clothing and was crying, crying endlessly. Her eyes were swollen, and she did not even raise her head to look at us. But when I mentioned Mezere, she turned to me and began looking at me very, very profoundly. This was an Armenian girl who had been kidnapped. These beautiful clothes had been given to her by a Turkish soldier, the claws of whom she was not yet free. When I spoke about Mezere, she finally believed that I was Armenian; then, she said only a few words:

Brother, won't you save me from this?

All the women standing around me echoed her, saying:

For the love of God, if you can, save this girl from the hands of that dog.

All of our medicine was used up, so the German officer and I went to the local government's central pharmacy. The street was paved with flagstone; women and children lay on both sides of the road, all the way from the pharmacy to at least fifteen minutes away by foot. Someone's stomach was bloated; someone's eyes were bandaged; another person was covered in wounds. A woman was spitting blood beside another woman, who had fallen from vertigo. Discolored, skeletal, afflicted by a thousand different pains and illnesses, this entire multitude of Armenians were fallen on the ground, each of them awaiting their turn to enter the pharmacy. Hundreds were also crowded right in front of the door.

Someone sighed; someone moaned; someone plaintively repeated *Allah khadru ichun (For God's sake)*; with supplications and entreaties similar to this, they begged for medicine; nonetheless, the pharmacy doors were shut and guarded by a soldier.

When the German soldier appeared, the Turkish guard became confused and began using his rod to split the gathered crowd into two, so that they can open a path for him. Under his blows, the half-dead population, covered in wounds, fell to both sides. Countless hostile eyes became fixed on the German officer I was with; it was as if their gazes hurled hatred and malediction. We hastily crossed the passage opened by the guard, and when we entered the pharmacy, we saw lips of all the Armenians there moving to yell something, but they could not speak. The German officer was deeply moved and reprimanded the Turkish soldier for his behavior, all the while regretting that he had come there himself.

We asked the pharmacist:

Do you have siwlfat te kinin?[2]

Confused, the pharmacist answered:

What did he say?

Solfato, solfato, I replied.

Right. We're out, I'm sorry.

Everything we wanted was either entirely used up or in very poor condition, and so, we left empty-handed.

On the road, we encountered a local Armenian, who said:

Forty to fifty people, mostly women, die every day due to a lack of medicine. The lowest-ranking gendarme, soldier, or local scoundrel has an Armenian girl at home, or an Armenian woman as a servant.

We departed from Deir ez-Zor on November 24.

---

[2] [AM] Armenian transliteration of the French *Sulfate de Quinine*, or *Quinine Sulfate*, an antimalarial medication.

20

Toward Anē.[1] Anē. An Old Man Loses Consciousness. The Market.

We changed our boatmen, taking on Arabs in Deir ez-Zor. They constantly talked about their roguery and the torments they had inflicted on Armenian girls. As we passed near a cliff on the bank of the river, one of the young boatmen saw a pregnant Armenian woman and jumped from the boat, intending to pursue her. But he suddenly lost his balance trying to climb a vertical part of the cliff, and he fell into the river. He was hardly able to get free from the intense current, and he was nearly dead when he did. When he finally came out of this, seeing this as a punishment from heaven, he made a vow to set free all the Armenian girls he was holding and to always endeavor to defend Armenians.

On December 3, we arrived at Anē. I had a letter to hand over to a deported Armenian living there. Although we did not need to stop at that port, the German officer I was traveling with ordered that our boats stop, so that I could deliver my letter. I immediately disembarked and saw a few Armenians trading eggs, bulgur, and other goods with the locals. Off in the distance, I saw a row of Armenians cleaning and dyeing skins. I met an old man with white hair, and reading the name and address written on the envelope, I asked him where I could find this person.

It's me, he said. Give me the letter. Is it from my sister?

Then, he fainted from the intensity of his emotions and fell to the ground.

---

[1] [MA, TMB] Anē, current day Karaağaç, is located north of Marash (current Kahramanmaraş). The city lies on a plain at the foot of Ahır Dağı (Mount Ahır). Zabel Yesayan renders this city as Անէյ (*Aney*) in the Armenian.

The German officer and I went to the market to purchase some things. Anē is a small town with a small market made up of only a few shops. There are also two bakeries here, built by Armenians, and a few commercial and artisan shops. The children also worked, selling various goods. We could not find yogurt in the market, but an Armenian woman brought us boxes of it herself.

21

Toward Hadise.[1] Hadise. The Price of Freeing an Armenian Girl.

We departed from Aney on December 4, having instructed our boatmen to buy an abundant of bread, since we would be traveling through sandy fields for three days straight. The desert here transforms completely into an arid and infertile space. The wind, which even creates waves on the river, causes intense sandstorms that make the air unbreathable.

Our bread ran out, and so, we stopped before a hamlet made up of only three houses and a caravanserai, which the government had newly established to defend the road. We tried to buy bread there, but we could only find flour. When I tried to enter one of the homes to have the bread baked, an older gendarme hastily blocked the entrance and did not let me enter. We went to other Arabs, who gladly took on the responsibility of baking the bread for us.

Our gendarmes also joined us. They had also bought flour and had given it to that old gendarme who blocked my entrance.

When it was time, one of the gendarmes in our group sent a small Arab girl over to the old gendarme and said:

Go, see if our bread is ready.

Returning, the little one said:
Mariam says they should wait a little longer.
Surprised, I asked:

There are Christians here?

I immediately went to the local gendarme's house; despite the opposition of the gendarmes I was traveling with, I entered. I saw the old man sitting beside an Armenian girl, about twenty years old; she was still wearing her traditional

---

[1] Hadise- Badgerazart Pnashkharhig Pararan, by H. S. Aprigean, places Hadise as part of Amid (Dickranagerd/Diyarbekir) near the Tigris towards Mosul.

clothing, from which I gathered that she was from Cilicia. And by the *tonir*,[2] there was another similarly dressed girl, who was nineteen years old. They were both sad, pensive, and sunburnt. I asked the old gendarme, who had stood up to greet me:

Who are these women?

He could not answer. Confused and afraid, the girls watched us, and it was as if they were silently beseeching us for aid.

Speaking in the name of my German officer, I told him that before we reached Baghdad, he had to return those girls to their parents, who had passed by three days ago.

When we returned to the local Arabs, I discovered that the old gendarme had taken these two girls as his wives.

Our boats set off soon after. That was the fastest and most dangerous point on the river. The vast fields of sand, which were the wind's playthings, were spread out on both sides. The sandstorms could be so intense that even local Arabs sometimes lost their way. The arid, fruitless sea of black and pale sand was storming.

On December 6, we arrived at Hadise. This was a small town in a beautiful oasis. The town's houses were arranged like an amphitheatre on the flank of an incline. Abundant date trees rose on both sides of the river. There were about 700 Armenians in this town, who occupied themselves with various jobs—although they all complained that there was little work. I had gone to buy yogurt, when I encountered an Armenian woman who was knitting a sock and crying.

Her eyes were nearly blinded by tears, but she continued knitting the sock, which she was close to finishing.

Are you selling that, mother?[3] I asked.

She let out a heartfelt *Oh . . . Oh . . .* and was unable to reply.

Her Arab neighbor explained the woman's sorrow. The local gendarme had taken her daughter and demanded a pair of socks for her safe return. The gendarme said:

Your daughter will stay with me for as long as it takes you to finish.

The woman hastened to finish the socks, her fingers cramping, and her heart weighed down by sorrow.

---

[2] [TN]: Cylindrical clay oven, usually underground.
[3] [MA, TMB] A common and informal way of addressing an older woman in Armenian.

22

Hīt.[1] The Students of Aintab's Seminary. The Market. An Armenian Girl Is Requested from Baghdad.

On December 8, we arrived at Hīt, which is a small city on the riverbank. Forests of date palms could be seen, among which adobe houses blended in. Everything here was abundant, especially dates. On the riverbank, I met two young Armenian men, who had been students at the seminary in Aintab. They addressed the German officer I was with and asked him to give them any kind of work. I asked them questions, and they said that there was no suitable work for them in the city. They said:

> If only we had learned to bake instead of getting an education! You see how we've come to the water's edge like this, hoping we can find work loading and unloading the boats, or doing something else.

They were in a state of extreme despair.

The market was in the city. One way or another, these Armenians had become settled, and they were occupied with different kinds of work. They were mostly *kebab* vendors and retailers. I asked one:

How is your situation here?

How . . . ? No more villages lie between here and hell . . .

On the road, I met Armenians busy building houses. They were making bricks from a mixture of soil and sand. There were skilled masons among them, who had prepared new kinds of cement from whatever materials they had at their disposal; this surprised the locals. Moving on from there, I arrived at the small square, where I saw many Armenian women seated in a circle sewing socks or doing other kinds of needlework. These women were also from Aintab.

---

[1] [MA, TMB] Hīt, also known as Heet, is a city that lies on the northwest of Ramādī, Iraq.

For the most part, the boatmen at the riverbank were Armenian, and they transported people or loads from one bank to the other. When I spoke with them, they said:

We're surviving, brother; but this isn't life, it's death.

I went to the telegraph office to send word ahead that we would be needing a cart in Fallujah.[2] The telegraph operator, who had just received a wire, slammed his fist impatiently on the table and exclaimed: *Again the same thing!*

I picked up the telegraph and read it. It said as such:

We are satisfied with your last delivery. Send another Armenian girl or woman.

The ones asking were government officials in Baghdad.

Spring had already arrived here. The lambs were born; the grass had grown to half its full height; and the vegetables had ripened. This was the best weather of the year; in the summer, the temperature reaches 48–50 degrees in the shade.

---

[2] [MA, TMB] Situated on the Euphrates River, Fallujah is a city in present-day Iraq. Under the Ottoman rule, it was a minor stop across the desert.

23

Ramadi.[1] 300 Armenians from Zeytun in a Cave. The Conduct of an Arab Baker. Fallujah. The Story of a Wealthy Armenian Family.

We arrived at Ramadi on December 9. It was a beautiful and fertile oasis. On the riverbank, there appeared date palms and orange trees. The fields had been cultivated, and there was greenery as far as the eye could see. The market was in the middle of the city, where there was also a caravanserai. Here the bakers and produce vendors were all Armenian; there were 300–400 Armenians from Cilicia. A local Arab told me that in a cave at the very edge of Ramadi, there were about 300 Armenians from Zeytun, who had been made to pass through the city. Their state was uncertain. *These were the bravest among the Armenians*, said the Arab.

I went to Ahmed Khebbez's home to buy bread, and I met a few Armenians from Aintab there who were also buying bread. I spoke with them. They complained about the lack of work; they were constantly waiting for the moment when they would be allowed to return to their homeland, even though the government had said that they would not return and had told them that they would be given the means to survive in Mesopotamia. This was their greatest sorrow.

> How come? Is it because the Arabs aren't good? Are you not able to live with them? Why do you want to needlessly return to your homeland?
> Yes, they said. The Arabs are good. But we cannot bear this life forever. We can't accept this country as our homeland. The fire burns only for those who are caught in it. Don't you have a homeland?
> And they sighed with all their hearts: *Oh . . . Oh . . .*
> When the Armenians left, I asked the Arab:
> Who are these people?

---

[1] [MA, TMB] The present-day city lies in the west of Baghdad and Fallujah, Iraq.

> Brother, he replied, you do not know what good people these are! These are Earmels.[2] I don't know why the government exiled them here. They say they revolted, that they're bad people, but we don't see anything like that. Quite the opposite: they are such good and modest people, that even now, I give them bread on credit. They owe me money, but I give it to them anyways. They are trustworthy people. I am confident that they'll pay me when they can.

I saw that the German officer was secretly taking the photograph of a group of unfortunate ones, even though we had been strictly forbidden from taking any photographs. I approached him and asked what he intended to do with the picture.

After the war, I'm going to expose this barbarity, he said.

We were walking together toward our boat when we saw gendarmes on the road selling rings. My officer wanted to buy something for his wife, but when he discovered that these objects had been plundered from Armenians, he returned them, saying:

I cannot buy them. I cannot even look at them.

We left Ramadi the same day, and on December 10, we arrived at Fallujah, where the portion of our journey along the river ended.

Fallujah is located on the left bank [of the Euphrates], which is connected to the right bank by a moveable bridge. This wooden bridge, which can be opened or closed at any point, sits on a row of circular rafts tied together with bark from palm trees and covered in tar.

The very wealthy Kuyumjian family resided in Fallujah, and the greater part of the city belonged to this family. There are flour mills, lime factories, and machines for distributing water—all of which belong to this same family. The city has a large market, a government building, a telegraph office, gardens, and dense date palms. There are also abundant fish.

I set off to find any of the Kuyumjians. A Jew malevolently told me:

---

[2] [AM] Yesayan and Toroyan use the original Arabic word that must have been used by this Arab himself, *Earmel* in Armenian transliteration, which means "widower," "destitute," "needy." There is nothing in the text that necessarily points to these individuals being widowers, and this would not have been the usual course of events during the genocide (the men were more often killed off and the women were left widowed), although it is entirely possible that these were men who made it to Ramadi without their families. Regardless, any deportees who had made it this far would have experienced substantial loss and would have been in a state of destitution, and this word holds the depth of this meaning.

They've all been driven out. Don't ask after them at all. Their homes, work: everything has been upended. They've put someone in charge of all their properties.

Where were they sent? I asked.

Mosul, he replied. And I think they killed them on the journey.

I later learned that the Jew's conjecture was false, and that they had reached Mesopotamia from Mosul.

In Fallujah, we handed the military equipment we had brought with us over to the military authorities. We took the money we had on us, and renting a cart, we departed on December 11.

24

Baghdad. Forty-nine Armenians Are Deported. The Gallows. The Armenians' Situation. The German Consul's Resistance. The Words of Halil Pasha.

We stayed in Baghdad for a few days. There I heard that forty-nine notable Armenians, locals and foreigners, had been deported to Mosul. They had arrived safely in Mosul and had just telegraphed the news that they were departing for Deir ez-Zor. On December 2, they had hanged a young man from Sepasdia with the last name Takaworian, who had supposedly been arrested for propagandizing among Arabs in favor of the British. A few Armenians remained imprisoned in Baghdad.

The remaining Armenians, who made up 200 homes, were safe for the time being.

I met a young man from Kharpert who, hearing that I had passed through the deportation centers in Mesopotamia, was inquiring about his mother. He had received the following letter from her:

> My dear son, they butchered your father in front of my very eyes. They sent your two brothers, your sister, and me here, among Arabs. As I write this letter, one of your brothers has died, while the rest of us are dying of starvation. If you don't send us aid quickly, we will not live much longer.

The boy was bewildered and extremely agitated. Like a caged lion, his powerlessness had made him lose his mind, since he did not know how to get help to his family.

Every day, Armenians from this or that village would approach me and ask for word about their village, their relatives, or about Armenians in general. Until that day, nobody had heard news about what was taking place upstream.

When I narrated to them what I had seen, they were besieged by horror and fright; turning to one among them, they said:

Hagop, are you prophet?

Hagop apparently had constantly been repeating this phrase:

> The taste of the Tigris has changed—it tastes like blood.

The German officer and I went to visit the German consul, who, upon seeing me, asked Mr. Otto Oehlmann:

> Your translator is Armenian? If he is, I strictly forbid you from taking him with you. I will find you another translator.

Although I did not know Persian, my officer had the confidence to say to the consul:

> This gentleman is a Lebanese Catholic Arab. He knows Persian very well. I am accustomed to him, and his loyalty has been tested. I ask that you officially accept him and give him papers to cross into Persia.

The consul, who looked at me suspiciously, rejected my officer's request.

When we returned to our room, Mr. Otto Oehlmann expressed sorrow for his failure. He said:

> I will take you up to the border, and I will use any means available to me to help you cross; but if we do not succeed, I am not responsible. Don't blame me. I trust you, and I know that no matter what happens, you will not hurt me.

I accepted his proposition.

Take me to the border, I said. I will find a way across.

He encouraged me and expressed his confidence that we would succeed. This German officer I was traveling with had always been magnanimous, generous, and noble toward me.

In Baghdad, I heard from a reliable source that Khalil Pasha had spoken at an Ittihadist club and said:

> I plucked out the heart of Armenia. Now it's the Arabs' turn. Whoever does not bow before the Ottoman crescent will be subjected to the same fate as the Armenians.

I heard, moreover, that the Turks had captured two damaged airplanes from the British. They wanted to repair them but could not find any Turks who could do the work and were instead forced to ask Armenians, all the while cursing their people's ineptitude. Those planes became operational with the help of those Armenians.

25

Toward Persia. The Arabs Steal Two Trunks of Weapons. We Cross the Border. The German Officer Takes to Illness. He Goes Mad. Toward Kermanshah.[1] The German Officer Commits Suicide. The Russians Capture Kermanshah, and I Go to the Caucasus.

On December 21, we departed from Baghdad. We were given arms and munitions captured from the British, and having loaded them on carts, we set off for Persia. Before we reached Baquba,[2] local Arabs took advantage of the fact that two of our carts were lagging behind and stole two trunks full of weapons. It was midnight when the cart drivers arrived and recounted to the German officer what had happened. The German officer became bewildered and deeply affected. He said:

> What am I going to do? I am completely disgraced. They'll say that I was unable to deliver all the weapons to their destination.

Seeing how agitated he was, I felt sorry for him, because I honestly liked him. I decided to save him from his panic, and I expressed that I would be willing to go and use any means necessary to retrieve the stolen weapons.

When he heard my proposal, his happiness knew no bounds. He immediately handed me 25 liras, as well as his pistol and dagger. He gave me permission to use these weapons without fear, if necessary. He took a horse from the drivers, handed it to me, and, at the moment of my departure, said:

---

[1] [MA, TMB] A city in the western part of Iran.
[2] [MA, TMB] Ba'qūbah is a city to the northeast of Baghdad, on the Diyala River. This city was turned into a refugee camp and housed many Armenians following the genocide of the Armenians in the Ottoman Empire.

Go, show us how brave you are! I know your people well. Do you remember when I told you that I wanted an Armenian interpreter, that I didn't want someone from any other race? You asked me why. Now the time has come for me to remind as to why.

Led by an Arab, I crossed the Nahr al-Ba'qūbah river by night. We cut through a vast field and went through a forest of date palms, at the other end of which appeared a field and thousands of tents.

When we became visible to them, a state of alarm took hold among the Bedouins, and every one of them plucked up their guns and approached us. We raised our arms to show that we had no ill intent, and upon our request, they led us to the sheikh. After greeting the sheikh, we humbly put our lives in his hands in accordance with Arab customs. The sheikh gave us his assurances by raising his finger. They offered us coffee, after which I expressed to the sheikh that men from his tribe had stolen two trunks of guns and ammunition; [I also stated] that this was an issue of honor for the German officer I was traveling with. The sheikh demanded that they bring the trunks to him, which they did quickly, but the trunks were empty. The guns, which had been distributed already, were collected and brought forth before us on the orders of the sheikh. The sheikh gave us two mules, on which we loaded the trunks; then, we set off accompanied by two of the Arabs from this tribe. I insisted on making a monetary gift to the sheikh, but he would not accept it. We settled for giving a few liras to the Arabs who accompanied us.

The German officer was waiting impatiently at the edge of the village. When he saw the full trunks being brought back by the thieves themselves, he kissed my forehead from joy, and pressing my hand, he said: *You have saved my honor.*

When we entered our room, he prepared tea and fruits; although we had four Afghan servants, he served me himself.

From Baquba, we traveled to Shahraban,[3] and from there to Hanike, where there was the first border post. We took mules in place of our carts. I saw that the German officer was looking for me excitedly. When I approached him, he said:

I have good news: crossing the border is easy. But nonetheless, we need to be careful.

And he arranged it as such the mule-drivers would cross first; then I would cross; and he would follow an hour later, so that he could save me in the event that I am stopped.

---

[3] [MA, TMB] The old name of the city Miqdadiyah, located in the northeast of Baghdad and Ba'qūbah.

The mules had already reached the border. I approached the local *mülazım* (lieutenant),[4] and presenting myself as someone with an official role, I requested gendarmes for the protection of our load. I explained to the lieutenant that if he did not help me, he would be seen as having worked against the empire's military needs, and that he would be held liable. The lieutenant said that the road was safe, but that he would provide me with as many gendarmes as was necessary.

Seeing that his attention turned toward something else, and that it would not even cross his mind to block my passage, I advanced without insisting for too long. We crossed the border this way, and on December 26, we arrived at the first post on the Persian side, at Qasr-e Shirin,[5] where the German officer I was traveling with joined me and congratulated me on escaping from the Turkish yoke.

We departed from Khaser Shirin for Sarpul;[6] there, in the early morning, we met a high-ranking German officer. He told Otto Oehlmann that he needed to make haste. The enemy was approaching, and he ordered the German officer to go to the battlefield immediately after delivering the arms and ammunition.

For this reason, Captain Otto Oehlmann arranged for me to oversee our caravan, to take it on as my responsibility; then, he told the Afghans that they were to obey my orders with regard to everything.

That day, however, the German officer again turned pensive and sad. He was very tired and dizzy. He was forced to lie on the bed and rest, and calling me over, he began speaking with nervous energy.

He remembered his parents, who were from Berlin; he remembered his childhood and spoke with intense fervor about his wife, who was also from Berlin but was in Tabriz at present. After traveling for a long time with his wife—because he had been the representative of a factory in Moscow—they had settled in Tabriz, where they had been acquainted with the European and Armenian communities. After the declaration of war, he had left his wife with the American consul and traveled through Baghdad to Istanbul. At the time of his departure, his wife was pregnant, and she had given birth to their first-born child in his absence. He received a picture of his son in Aleppo. He spoke with a heavy heart about his exhaustion and agitation. All the horrific things he had seen were coming back to him.

After seeing those women and children, how am I going to look at my Luise and my child with a tranquil heart? he asked anxiously.

---

[4] [MA, TMB] The equivalent rank of a lieutenant in the armed forces of the late Ottoman Empire.
[5] [MA, TMB] A border town in the province of Kermanshah, Iran.
[6] [MA, TMB] Also known as Sarpole Zahâb, a city in Kermanshah province, Iran.

Nonetheless, we had to leave the next day, and on December 28, we arrived in Suq Haradize,[7] where the German captain's temperature rose intensely; there, he was forced into bedrest once again. He said to me:

I have complete faith in your loyalty, and I trust you, even with my life.

The German officer had still not fully recovered, when we were forced to leave for Kerend,[8] where the German ambassador in Tehran found us in the middle of the night and pressingly ordered us to leave immediately and deliver the arms to Kermanshah. That night went very badly for Otto Oehlmann; he spoke ceaselessly and emotionally about the horrific things we had seen in Mesopotamia. At times, he would go silent, then he would suddenly call out his wife's name: Luise, Luise . . . He associated the painful impressions he had borne with his wife and newborn child in an astonishing manner.

It seems I will not succeed in seeing my wife and child, he said.

On December 30, we arrived in Harunabad.[9] On the second day, his fever intensified, and he began to talk idly. When someone would come and visit him, he would stand up and say: *The Kaiser has come*. He would undress, throw everything he had around the room, and shout threats. Then, he would call me over.

I have gone mad, pay me no mind, he said.

His delusions would recommence, or he would play attentively for hours with a splinter of wood or a fallen thread.

Seeing that it was no longer possible for him to travel in his condition, I wrote a letter to the German consul in Kermanshah, saying that I, Otto Oehlmann's translator, desired to inform him that the German officer I was with had become extremely ill, and that he was in a maddened state. I requested a doctor and for an officer to be sent to collect the arms and money. And after nightfall, giving my Afghan servant a lira as gratuity, I sent the letter.

No one had come by nightfall by the second day. The German officer had almost entirely lost his mind, and he spoke openly of suicide. I took his guns and moved them elsewhere. On the rare occasions that he came back to himself, he would force me to sleep in his room.

It is possible that I will die, he said. But don't be afraid, I will not harm you.

I had a gendarme stand at the door as a guard, and I remained by my officer's side.

---

[7] [MA, TMB] A city in Iran.
[8] [MA, TMB] Also known as Kerend-e Garb, a city in Kermanshah province.
[9] [MA, TMB] A village in the Haradan province, Iran

At night, I heard a cart outside. This was purely a coincidence. A German engineer, who had broken his leg after falling from a considerable height, was returning from Kirmanshah. I went and explained everything to him; he accompanied me with a stretcher to Otto Oehlmann's bedside. The engineer wanted to speak with him, but the German officer was in a state of delirium and understood nothing; he wanted to give him medicine, but the officer furiously refused. At that point, the engineer, pulling me aside, said that he would take care of everything; he also wrote the following note:

> Hand the munitions and everything you have over to the local Persian gendarmes, and without revealing what is in the trunks, depart immediately for Kirmanshah, because Captain Otto Oehlmann has a severe fever, which has affected his mind, and this could cause things to get extremely dangerous.

I immediately arranged for a cart to be brought; after clothing him, with great difficulty, we set off, leaving everything there in Harunabad. The night was very dark and cold; the snowy road was uneven, and he was speaking idly, a completely delirious patient raving incessantly. In the morning on the second day, we came across the doctor from the German hospital and a soldier, who had come to meet us; they immediately took Otto Oehlmann to the hospital. They also procured a room for me in the city.

Captain Otto Oehlmann had improved slightly in the hospital and wanted to see me. When I presented myself to the local German consul to hand over the papers I was holding, he immediately sent me to him, saying that I was urgently wanted. The doctor and I agreed that I should stay with my officer until he recovered. When the captain saw me, it was as if he were entirely healed. He sat up in his bed and began complaining about how rough the hospital attendants were. We decided that I would spend the night in his room, and on the following morning, the doctor examined him and told me that my presence had made a significant difference in his amelioration; he requested that I stay.

But the behavior of the hospital administrator toward me was uncivil and insupportable. She refused to give me food; she considered me a servant and thought she could order me to do her lowliest work. Hurt by this, I asked the German officer to allow me to at least leave at night, and I promised to visit him every day. The illness had almost entirely disappeared already, and he was no longer delirious. He even thought about the fact that I might not have any money on me and had arranged for me to take as much as I needed from his own purse, which was held by the doctor. I returned all the papers he had given me, including his diary, where he had written his impressions every day. To be safe,

I refrained from returning his guns. On the final night, he urgently demanded them and began to yell:

These people are going to kill me. I need to defend myself.

But he quickly calmed down again; and whispering Luise a few times, he fell asleep.

As I departed, I told the doctor that he had had thoughts of suicide, and that it was absolutely necessary to leave someone by his side at night.

Early the following morning, the hospital attendant sees that the patient, having donned his military uniform and official cap, having placed his Persian medal to his breast, has descended to the hospital courtyard and is looking for his sword. Unable to find what he is looking for, he returns to his room, and tying his sword belt, which he did have on him, around his neck, he fastens the other end to the bar at the top of a small door, and although he is quite tall, he brings his legs up off the ground and hangs himself and dies.

Despite his delirious state, he had not forgotten during the hours when he was better, and especially during those final days, to leave positive testimony about me in his journal. And he never revealed that I was Armenian.

On the following day, a fittingly honorable funeral procession took place. I followed the coffin to the cemetery. They placed his sword and hat in the coffin and buried him. The Russian army was advancing on Kangavar.[10] The Turkish army had also reached Kermanshah. They needed me as a translator and sent me to German officers, who were with the Turkish army. We departed for Sahneh,[11] from where the Turks began their assault on Kangavar, which the Russians had already occupied.

They took Kangavar, but under pressure from a large Russian force, we retreated to Karagözlü.[12] I wanted to escape here; pretending I was sick, I slept in a Persian caravanserai, whose owner, thinking I was a Muslim, wanted to take me to his house.

The Kurds at the vanguard of the Ottoman army, who were on the point of abandoning Kangavar, entered the caravanserai; seeing me there, they quickly informed the Turkish army, which was at the foot of a nearby mountain. A few mounted gendarmes came and, believing that I was a Muslim and sick, took pity on me and took me to Karagözlü. There was a Persian there who had just died. There was no imam, so they asked me to read the Qur'an, which I did.

---

[10] [MA, TMB] A city in the Kermanshah province in Iran.
[11] [MA, TMB] A city in the Kermanshah province in Iran.
[12] [MA, TMB] Armenian transliteration of yüzbaşı, lieutenant in the Ottoman/Turkish army.

While with that force, I heard Hasan Effendi yüzbashi[13] say:

If you capture any Armenian prisoners, kill them where they stand, without taking them to the Germans.

The Russian assault was intensifying. On February 19, we began retreating, and on February 22, we arrived in Kermanshah.

Considering this an opportune moment, I wanted to hide in Kermanshah, even though the German officers, in dire need of interpreters, made me other grand promises. But taking advantage of the confusion of retreat, I took refuge in a Christian's home, giving him payment. By nightfall, the Russians had occupied the heights of Kermanshah, and the Turks had already retreated. Emerging from my hiding spot, I encountered two Russian soldiers for the first time. When I said I was Armenian and was looking for other Armenians, they pointed to a field, which I went to immediately. There I met Armenian officers and Khan Kurken Saghnakhski Uzbashian. They welcomed me with open arms and offered me all kinds of comforts. I served for four months in the Russian army as a censor; during that time, I had already begun to send my impressions to the *Arev* periodical in Baku. My painful journey had shot my nerves, and requesting leave, I departed for the Caucasus.

Zabel Yesayan
Translated by Arakel Minassian

---

[13] [TN] *yüzbaşı* in Turkish, this is a military title meaning that this officer is at the head of a hundred soldiers.

Afterword: Testimony and Authorship
Zabel Yesayan's *The Agony of a People*[1]
Written by Marc Nichanian, translated by Tamar M. Boyadjian

The Agony of a People is the first in-depth offering, in the Armenian language, about the events of 1915 and about the Armenians who were exiled in Mesopotamia,[2] narrated by an eyewitness and printed in the press as the first extensive work of its kind. It was published in Baku, in *Kordz* (*Labor*) monthly in the February and March 1917 issues. The name of the eyewitness survivor was Haig Toroyan, and the stories he narrated were penned by Zabel Yesayan. Across 150 pages, Toroyan narrates what he saw—the frightful events that occurred around him—from 1914 to the early years of 1916. The opening [of the book] includes the two-page, jolting prologue of Zabel Yesayan, where she writes: "painfully imbued with the duty that fell upon me, I regarded it as sacrilege to make the subject of a literary work the suffering throes of death of an entire people."

Along with the imperative to inscribe, there is also, as a result, the desire to *resign* oneself from the literary. [To do this] not only for Armenians but also in the face of the entire world, no one before Zabel Yesayan had realized this need, nor [had anyone] formalized such a thing out loud through a work that broke the boundaries of literature. She defends the rights of a new type of narrative—a genre that was not referred to as "testimony" at that time. As such, what Zabel Yesayan produces is a revelation, a revelation for a work that did not exist before it, an incomprehensible undertaking of a two-sided nature, which

---

[1] I would like to thank Dr. Maral Aktokmakyan and Jennifer Langley for their comments on an earlier version of this translation.
[2] [TMB] Dr. Nichanian uses the same term that Zabel Yesayan does in the book to refer to the region "between the two rivers," that is the within the Tigris-Euphrates system as "Mesopotamia." I have chosen to use this translation to keep consistently with the term Dr. Nichanian uses, upon which Minassian has also relied. It is important to note, however, that this does not refer to the ancient region of the Sumerians and Akkadians (including the Assyrians and Babylonians), but rather the historical region that includes present-day Iraq and parts of Iran, Kuwait, Syria, and Turkey.

is the undertaking of "testimony." Why two-sided? Because [testimony] requires the use of the literary, just as much as it must resigns itself from being literary.[3]

Zabel Yesayan was the only woman who was on the blacklist of [intellectuals, thinkers, writers, and such important Armenian figures on] April 24. She was not arrested and spent the coming months moving from one hiding place to another, living the underground life of a fugitive. At that time, her mother and her five-year-old son resided in Constantinople, while her husband and daughter lived in Paris. It was only at the end of July that she finally succeeded in fleeing to Bulgaria, and it was only later that she was able to bring her mother and her son to her, in Sofia. But, even there, she was not able to remain long. In October of 1915, Bulgaria became involved in the military advancements of the Germans, supporting them, and in turn, Turkey. As such, Yesayan then moved on with her son to the Caucasus. In the Caucasus, Yesayan gave lectures, but especially started the long-term undertaking of working with survivors. The exact details of this work have remained unknown to us until recently. The only knowledge we had came to us through her letters. Now, we have a clearer idea of her work during this time, primarily because of testimonies that have been published in Yerevan in the last several years, among the series entitled *Vshdabadum* [*A Book of Grieving*].

It is necessary to recall that in 1911, Yesayan—in an Armenian of the twentieth century—published one of the most notable books written in Armenian entitled, Աւերակներու Մէջ [*Averagneru Mech; In the Ruins*], where she provides an account of her convictions of the 1909 massacres of Adana—from the daybreak [the massacres started] through the three months she remained there. Written in 1911, this book was already a form of witnessing—in modern terms, a testimony. There, [in this book], this woman of letters, addresses her "fellow countryfolk," the Turks, when she explains how the victims died for the freedom of their people. In all cases, this was a paradox; even so, it was not until recently that the Turks had the chance to read Zabel Yesayan's reflections, in 1911, and to be convinced of the humanity of these victims—to be convinced that they had been sacrificed for them, to protect their civil rights. The truth is that after 1915, Yesayan was not able to express herself the same way: she was not able to engage in the same type of works of mourning; she was not able to present testimony as a measure of citizenship—a means through which citizenship could be instigated or revived.

---

[3] The *Agony of a People* has been reprinted one time (greatly abridged) by Levon Mesrob in his 1952 book printed in Paris, Genocide and Rebirth (Արիւն եւ վերածնունդ), with a new title *The Testimony of Haig* (Հայկ Թորոյեանի վկայութիւն), simply signed "Written down by Zabel Yesayan"—and of course with the disappearance of the signature "Zabel Yesayan." [This] maintains a neutrality not only for the work of the author but also for the յայտնագործութիւն, around which I speak of here.

"The principle of citizenship" was no longer valid.[4] And so, Yesayan never wrote a testimony, in first person, that is even comparable to the one she composed in 1911. What did she do instead? For three years, continuously, she dedicated her time to survivors: to collecting their testimonies; to recording them, to rectifying them, publishing them, and translating them to French. Here is what she writes to Chobanian [in this regard]:

> I have been engaged in the task of organizing all these documents and testimonies relating to the latest persecutions that have reached us from Turkish-Armenia [Ottoman Empire]. In its essence, the work is extremely painful; as a result, my nervous system is completely disrupted; but, at all costs, I will complete the task. After I categorize everything, I have the intention of preparing a general study [of the material], which will most likely be printed in Kordz monthly—that is, if I am still alive. . . . Take into account that I have been spending ten to twelve hours a day reading and arranging horrific stories regarding people being ravished and massacred [!].[5]

And so, Toroyan's testimony was the first expansible testimony that was ever printed in the Armenian press. The survivor, Haig Toroyan, traveled the Euphrates from November 1915 to January 1916, from Jarābulus to Baghdad, as the assistant and translator of a German officer. One by one, he saw with his own eyes, the concentration camps—that were constructed and being constructed—on the edges of the Euphrates. He and the German officer photographed what they had seen there, and both had successively recorded their convictions in their journals. The name of the German officer was Otto Oehlmann. The German officer was not able to tolerate what he had seen. When they reached Iran—where they were meant to turn over the guns and ammunition they were transporting—Otto Oehlmann became delirious and eventually committed suicide. Toroyan, then, crossed over to the Russian side, serving in the Russian army for some time as a translator once again. After which, he left the army, traveling to Tbilisi and Baku. He even went as far as having his eyewitness reports put into print in *Arev* [*Sun*] newspaper in Baku. He assigned the task of recording his entire story to Zabel Yesayan.

---

[4] With regard to the "inception of citizenship," I direct the reader to my introduction in the reprinted edition of *In the Ruins* (Aras, 2010). This was the first time the book was reprinted in over a hundred years. It includes not only Yesayan's blazing testimony but also a hardly familiarized article, published in four parts, in the summer of 1911 in the New York-based periodical Arakadz, where Yesayan speaks of things she had not—or perhaps she even could not say—in her book. The book has also been published in Turkish translation (Aras, 2014).

[5] Zabel Yesayan, *Letters*, Yerevan, 1977, page 146. The letter is dated "Dec. 1917," which is possibly incorrect.

Haig Toroyan was born in 1892—if we are to believe his Syrian passport. If his birthdate is correct, then in 1915 he would have been twenty-three years old. He was born in Aleppo. During that time, the long-standing Armenian community of Aleppo was comprised of mostly Arabic speakers. Most likely, the Toroyan family had, in comparison, more recently taken refuge in Aleppo—probably in the nineteenth century[6]—because Haig Toroyan not only spoke Armenian but also had a handle on Turkish, Kurdish, and Arabic. It was only because he knew Arabic well that he was able to pass himself off as both a Christian-Arab and as a translator during his travels with the German officer. His Arabic was beyond conversational. We know this because in the final pages [of his testimony] he explains how in Iran—due to the absence of a certain *imam*—he was asked to read the Qur'an during the funeral of a Muslim villager. Through Yesayan's pen, from start to finish, Haig Toroyan first describes the events of the year 1914 in Diyarbakır, where he attests his presence as a place he bought and traded antiques. He describes the first killings that took place in the city, the burning of the marketplace, and the persecutions. At the end of 1914, he moves from Diyarbakır to Jarābulus. Today, Jarābulus is located in the north of Syria. Back then, what made this city distinct was that the two main routes used to deport the Armenians crossed through it. It was both on the edge of the Euphrates, and, at the time, one of the stops of the unfinished Berlin–Baghdad railway. And so, starting from May of 1915, Toroyan saw those caravans of survivors who arrived there—sometimes these were only women, who had withered away to simply skin and bones. He saw those arriving by train and the heart-wrenching events that took place around the Jarābulus station. He also saw, for three consecutive months, from June to August, the corpses that ran down the Euphrates. Therefore, the first part of the testimony is comprised of all these events that took place in Diyarbekir and Jarābulus. Toroyan does not reveal to us the reasons or the conditions that brought him to Jarābulus. Under what circumstances or under what employment was he there? We do not know. Here, we turn to the writing we have from Jennifer Langley:

> Our family history tell us that he was the manager of a hotel located in the center of Aleppo (Bab al-Faraj), and that his younger brother Aram was the director of the Muslimiyeh train station which was located twelve kilometers from Aleppo. Haig would keep Armenians at the hotel and would help them to leave Syria

---

[6] [TMB] According to Jennifer Langley, the Toroyan family moved from Arapkir to Aleppo likely in the 1870s, as Haig's parents were married in Aleppo in 1880. Jennifer Langley is the great-granddaughter of Haig Toroyan's sister Armenouhi Toroyan Manoogian, who settled in Watertown, Massachusetts.

at night by train. The Ottoman Empire had their suspicions. As a result, he was forced to leave Aleppo. He spent the rest of his life in Iran. He was never married, and he had no children.[7]

And Levon Mesrob writes the following:

> Before the end of the war, Haig Toroyan returns to Mesopotamia in disguise, so that he may organize the liberation of the remaining Armenians. He is arrested and sentenced to death, escaping [the verdict] through a miracle. During the armistice, he returns to Aleppo devoting himself to the safekeeping of orphans. He opens Aleppo's Cilician School, [taking in] hundreds of students. The school, lacking the finances [to remain open, eventually] closes down. Haig Toroyan has been established in Tehran for the last twenty five years.[8]

We have almost no additional information about the life and efforts of Haig Toroyan. We know that around the middle of the year 1916, Toroyan was in the Caucasus. His narration in first person runs until February of 1916, and his meeting with Zabel Yesayan must have happened in the same year, in June. And so, the only information that we have, which is certain, is the details he gives us in his testimony—and he only mentions in his testimony his life in Jarābulus and his departure from there. He had gotten the attention of the local authorities because of all the help he had brought to those who were exiled. His life was in danger—but all this happens in Jarābulus, and not in Aleppo. And so, it is here that his report changes its position from its first person [narration]. Toroyan is introduced to the German soldier; he is then hired as an assistant and translator, after which they travel together along the Euphrates, with a company of Turkish soldiers. [They had the task of] transporting and turning over guns and ammunition that had been shipped to Istanbul to the German battalion—first in Baghdad, then in Iran. They departed on November 25, 1915, which falls on November 12 on the old calendar. They reached Baghdad at the end of December. This means that they traveled for a month and a half down the Euphrates. It was on this horrific journey that they saw, one by one, the deported gathered or dispersed at the edge that river. And these people, whom Toroyan and Otto Oehlmann saw that November and December of 1915, were the women and the elderly that were gathered at the newly built stations—most likely the remaining survivors of those caravans brought in from the highlands.

---

[7] Personal information received from Jennifer Langley, the daughter of the grandchild of Haig Toroyan's sister Armenouhi, who settled in Watertown.

[8] Genocide and Revival, page 16.

Haig Toroyan and Otto Oehlmann had only seen the early stages of the camps that were found along the Euphrates. When six months later, in June of 1916, Toroyan conveys his eyewitness account to Zabel Yesayan, he could not have known the fate of the Armenians who had been gathered there. The large-scale massacres in Deir ez-Zor had not begun just yet. It would take five months for [the Turks] to be able to wipe out all the Armenians they had collected in Deir ez-Zor; this was later from May to November of 1916. For this very reason, it is astonishing to learn from those pages that describe how—when in January of 1916—Haig Toroyan and Otto Oehlmann reach Dier ez-Zor, [Toroyan reports] that they find themselves in a small, quaint city where Armenians were, more or less, living together. Did I already mention that during their journey, both Toroyan and the German officer took photographs of what they saw and, so it seems, recorded their impressions, day by day, in a diary? Among other things, Toroyan had a series of diaries, which he had shown in June of 1916 to the French journalist Henry Barby—and we will discover under what circumstances. At the beginning of Zabel Yesayan's account [of Toroyan's testimony], she establishes the following in a footnote, where she writes: "In these pages, the story is written in first person because these are the descriptions and impressions of Mr. Haig Toroyan, which were described to me by word of mouth, and which then I recorded." Here, Zabel Yesayan wanted to leave the impression that she is merely the recorder [of Toroyan's words]. As such, this simple acknowledgment can be read as an effort to remain loyal to the words of an eyewitness and to shun away from embellishments in the text, as a way of remaining true to [the testimony] when documenting it. The matter is, however, that it is not the signature "Haig Toroyan" which appears at the end of the two parts of the "Agony of a People" printed in the periodical *Kordz*; rather [it is the signature] "Zabel Yesayan." Even though the testimonies of an eyewitness should not become subject to literary criticism, what is put into place, nevertheless, is the question of authorship. What Yesayan accomplished here was beyond the mere work of a recorder.

Wasn't it so that Toroyan himself did not know how to write? He does, however, have published reports signed with his name. In the final lines of his testimony printed in *Kordz*, he says the following: "I served in the Russian army for four months as a censor; and even, during that time, I began to send over my observations to the *Arev* newspaper in Baku"—meaning from February to June of 1916. Toroyan has three pieces that bore his signature, which, as such, make an appearance in *Arev* (the newspaper's entire collection can be found in the National Library of Yerevan). The first is a long report, printed in five consecutive issues (April 1 to April 7). Then, two other pieces, from August 27 to November 8. The titles of these are as follows: "Mesopotamia and The State of Armenians in Mesopotamia and Syria"; "The Basket of Turkey" *Հոլկահալի զամբիղը*; "Armenian Maidens" *Հայ կոյսերը*. The first series includes a preface from the editors:

> Hereinafter, we have an interesting letter written by an Armenian doctor from Kermanshah, [who has witnessed] from the banks of the Euphrates, from Aleppo to Baghdad, the deportations and dispersement of Armenians. The doctor has personally passed through stations filled with Armenians, who have been sadly persecuted, and promises to subsequently send his observations [of the events] to *Arev*.

As far as I know, Toroyan was not a doctor. He did, however, have reason to present himself as one. This series, printed in April 1916, is written in a language which is a mixture of both Western and Eastern Armenian. This leads us to believe that [these words] bear some sort of intervention on the part of the editors of *Arev*. What is presented to us, regarding the events around 1915, is comprised of a confusing compilation of notations—from the solitude of Jarābulus, from someone who received information from the periphery.

The second piece is completely different in nature. It is a literary piece written in a Western Armenian which finds its language lacking in certain parts. In two pages, it narrates the story of a merchant from Ras al-Ayn who saves children by secretly transporting them to Aleppo in baskets. This piece is literary in that it focuses on a particular character—whether real or fictional—weaving a new tale around them, and bringing their story to some sort of tragic ending. The merchant takes his last breath as he laments the death of those starving, young children in Aleppo. This same story can be found in the first section of *The Agony of a People*—penned and narrated by Zabel Yesayan in a more gradual, more impactful way, and exempt from a literary veiling, which among other thing, does not include [the implementation of] crafty descriptions that appear at the end of the story. It would require a well-informed writer to renounce the story from its literary elements, so as to leave the impression that the narrated tale was based on real-life events.

The third piece is written in an unblemished Western Armenian—most likely passing through the hands of Zabel Yesayan—and narrates the events around the pillaging and violence committed, one night, by a group of Circassians. This scene makes an appearance in the larger testimony—where the details are provided to their full extent—and shares the same language as the piece that is published in *Arev*. These three pieces are all signed "Haig Toroyan."[9] As so, we have here, a written piece which is almost entirely the same as what had

---

[9] Only that in the third piece the name is written wrong and appears as "Haig Toryan."

been published in both *Arev* and *Kordz*: signed there as "Haig Toroyan" and here as "Zabel Yesayan" [respectively]. It is the uncertainty of testimony that is at work here, regardless of its characters. It operates not only with regard to the signatures [it holds]—and thus its degree of authorship—but also to its degree of being "literary." One can only move away from the literary by being literary. And so, returning to *The Agony of the People,* if the intention of a piece of writing is to make an impression upon its reader, [and it does this only through the description of] horrific events—as in through only recording events, scenes, and impressions of real-life events—then the work is forced to rely upon literary elements to reach its desired result. This means that it has to slow its pace, bring actors to the stage, and organize an entire production by setting up the scene, to which titles can be assigned. The trafficking of children in front of the station at Jarābulus. The night-pillaging of a caravan. The caravanserai in Nusaybin. The girl who committed suicide at Meskene.

In addition to this question [we keep coming back to] of being forced to continually resign from the literary, there is yet another matter, which transforms this one testimony into something exceptional of its kind. Zabel Yesayan, who knew French perfectly, never once considered translating this writing of hers into French. Why is the question of translation being raised here, all of a sudden? In the most explicit way, Zabel evokes the human conscience and consciousness, directing [her work] toward civilized people and imagining a foreign reader. Let us recall what she mentions in her preface, in this regard:

> What an Armenian or other reader may find in this inscription is beyond any type of imaginable hell. One can say for certain that in the horrors of these world wars—when almost everywhere, the emotions of all people have become dull, shocked and effected by these misfortunes—the suffering of the Armenian people is in such a current state that it will amaze all of humanity and through the terror and the horror [that they are suffering] it can stir up the world's conscience.

This is yet another facet of the complicated workings of the inner contradictions of testimony and testimonials. We do not know who the author is. We don't know if what we are reading is a piece of literature or a document. We don't even know how the conscience of "all peoples" will be stirred up by these horrors and terrors if the original [text of this recorded testimony] is in Armenian. For this reason, the question of translation is put forth. Earlier, we read a section from Chobanian's letter written in Baku, where Yesayan says the following: "Take into account that I spent ten to twelve hours a day reading and arranging all types of stories regarding people being ravished and massacred." It is important to note that from the beginning of the year 1916 to the beginning of the year 1918—during her years in the Caucasus—Zabel Yesayan's main task was to collect and organize the testimony of survivors. We know this from her letters. Until recently, we had no real idea what exactly that work entailed. It is only in recent years that the matter became clarified: when Amatuni Virabyan, the director of the National Archives, and his colleagues published a volume entitled *Vshdabadum*. In the brief introduction to this volume, we discover that in Baku, in those years, a committee of six people were formed, initiated by the A.R.F. [Armenian Revolutionary Federation]. Their mission was to gather stories from survivors to the best of their ability. That is to say, they were not trying to have [the survivors speak of their experience] at length, but rather aimed to collect brief and succinct answers by following a list of questions formulated in advance (What village do you come from? How many people live there? In what year did the deportations start? How and under what conditions did you experience the annihilation? How did you survive?).[10] Ultimately, the goal was to prepare a voluminous immense collection made up of testimonies that carried the weight of [official] documents (each testimony contained the name of the survivor and the identity of the participants as authenticating elements, a type of guarantee). Then to take that pile of documents and send them to Paris, in hope that one day peace would be declared and the fate of the wronged would be investigated. But in that case, an organized jury—whether real or imaginary—would naturally not know how to read Armenian. For that reason, that entire collection of documents would have to be translated—translated to French, in fact—in order to be accessible: this is not something that appeals to the conscience of all common people, but to future members of a committee for peace. Who could have translated these to French? Who did they have in their company that could take on such a task? Of course, that would be Zabel Yesayan. So now, we know, what [is meant by] "stories about destruction, violence, and all sorts of shuddering events," of which Yesayan speaks in her letters addressed to Chobanian. For two years straight, Yesayan engaged herself in this work. When it came to the translation of these documents, the task is, yet again, entrusted to Zabel Yesayan—but it is not only that she read, organized, and translated

---

[10] The newly formulated series [is named as follows]: The Armenian Genocide in Ottoman Turkey. The Testimony of Survivors. Archival Documents, 3 volumes (Yerevan, 2013). During the invasion / undertaking known as "Vshdamadum," all the collected testimonies [of the Armenian Genocide] were brought together and presented for the first time to the public, in their entirety (the 2005 volume only offers a selection). The preface to the first volume individually names all those who participated in the invasion, and the preparation of the questionnaire is described in great detail.

them but also that she had the responsibility of transporting them to Paris.[11] Yesayan left Baku in May of 1918. Going through Tehran, then Basra and Cairo, she eventually reaches Paris in September of 1918—almost after six months of traveling. She brings with her the collection of documents—the questionnaires, documentary evidence, the translations, and photographs—among which there was most likely the photographs that Toroyan had taken during the time he was traveling along the Euphrates.

And there is more, and that more is truly shocking. In her letter addressed to Chobanian, Yesayan also states:

> Outside of those hours, I spend my time, about two hours a day, with Henry Barby. I count my free time in minutes and not in hours, because I am in a situation that I must finish my assumed task. Who knows what can happen? Any kind of danger could be a threat to those valuable papers: an investigative search, a fire, theft, etc. etc . . .

This Henry Barby was a French journalist, the correspondent for the French newspapers in the Caucasus. He is the author who published in Paris, the 1917 book entitled, *Au Pays de l'épouvante* (of course, after Toynbee and Lepsius), which describes the atrocious acts committed against the Armenians, obviously for the French public, if not also with the intent of shaking up the conscience of humanity. It is a well-known work.[12] What is not so well-known, however, is that Barby worked with Zabel Yesayan. Every day—for week, for months—it was Zabel who had translated for him those documents and testimonies into French, and it was from these translations that Barby would write his articles and eventually his book. It is also fair to say, without exaggeration, that from 1916 to 1922, whatever has been published in French about the fate of the Armenians has one way or another, without exception, gone through the hands of Zabel Yesayan. Upon her return to Paris, Zabel had undertaken two other tasks—she was translator into French of Palazzo Captain's book, *Tzavag* [*Agony*] (the book was published in 1919 under the title *Mémoires d'une déportée arménienne*, and only in the next year, in 1920, was the book published in Armenian—that is, in its original language—in New York). She was also the translator into French of

---

[11] In the introduction of the new volume, there is a letter by Rostom, one of the leaders of the ARF, addressed to his friends in Egypt. In it, we find a lucrative statement: "Mrs. Zabel will tell you more about our situation. . . . The Mrs. is bringing with her information around 'Vshdabadum.' You must use it for a larger propaganda campaign. The Mrs. is working on it." (page 8).

[12] The book was reprinted in recent years. See Henry Barby, *Au Pays de l'épouvante, l'Arménie martyre*, éditions du Cercle d'Ecrits Caucasiens, La Ferté-sous-Jouarre, with an introduction by Raymond Kévorkian. An Armenian translation was also published by Mikael Shamdanjian, In the Land of Horror (Constantinople, 1919); reprinted, Beirut, 1965.

Armenuhi Teotig's collection of testimonies of women survivors.[13] Yes. All of this has passed through the hands of Zabel Yesayan as a translator, but not *The Agony of a People*—or at least it seems that way.

And here comes the next surprise. For a long time, we believed that Haig Toroyan's name had only made an appearance on the pages of *Kordz* monthly, and subsequently in *Arev* newspaper in Baku; as such, [we believed], it had never appeared in other languages before the eyes of civilized society—that is to say, it had never been translated. This is inaccurate. A lecture that Zabel Yesayan gave in Paris in 1922 has been published in one of the volumes of the *Revue des Etudes Arméniennes* with the title, "Le rôle de la femme arménienne pendant la guerre."[14] What is narrated here in French can be found, word for word, in the memories of Toroyan, prepared by the hand of Yesayan. It can also be found in French in a published article written by Henry Barby in 1916. Of course, Toroyan's name had appeared earlier in French and English to the eyes of civilized society. If a reader were to open the book prepared by the hand of Toynbee, *Blue Book*—published in July of 1916—they will find that document number 144 bears the following title: "Exiles on the Euphrates: Record, dated Erzurum, June 1915, by M. Henry Barby, of an interview with Dr. H. Toroyan, an Armenian physician formerly in the service of the Ottoman Army; published in "Le Journal" of Paris, July 13, 1916.[15] Yes, this is indeed our Haig Toroyan—but here he is presented as a physician (just as he was at the beginning of the first series of his writings printed in *Arev*) and lo and behold, a doctor serving in the Ottoman army. The title of the article which appears in the Paris journal *Le Journal* is entitled, "Le camp des supplices et de la mort" ["The camp of torture and death"]. [It appears] with two photographs, an Armenian woman who supposedly escapes from a group of Turkish executioners and from a group of Chechens. Here is this reporter's introduction, translated by myself into Armenian:[16]

---

[13] The first: *Mémoires d'une déportée arménienne* (Paris: Flinikowski, 1919); the second: *Témoignages inédits sur les atrocités commises en Arménie, suivis d'un récit de l'épo-pée arménienne de Chabin-Karahissar, Dubreuil, Frèrebeau et Cie* (Paris, 1920).

[14] Revue des Etudes arméniennes, first series, vol. 2, 129–30.
Translator's Note: For an English translation of this, see: Meriam Belli, "Zabel Yesayan, 'Chronicle—The Role of the Armenian Woman during the War,'" *Journal for the Society of Armenian Studies* 28, no. 2 (April 2022): 220–34.

[15] James Bryce and Arnold Toynbee, *The Treatment of Armenians in the Ottoman Empire, 1915-1916: Documents Presented by Viscount Grey of Falloden by Viscount Bryce*, uncensored edition, ed. and with an introduction by Ara Sarafian (Princeton, NJ: Gomidas Institute, 2000), 568; entire document on pages 568–70.

[16] An Armenian translation of Barby's article has been published in the Paris newspaper *Artzakank*, July 25, 1916, with the tile "The camp of torture and death" (I assume the word is "camp").
Translator's Note: What Dr. Nichanian is referring to as the end of this note is the misspelling in the Armenian of the word camp where բանակատորդ (a misspelling) appears instead of the assumed բանակատեղը (lit. "the place of the army").

> Along the burning banks of the distant Euphrates, between sultry Mesopotamia and the Badiest-esh-Sham, the desolate desert of Syria, are encamped several thousands of deported Armenians who have escaped a great massacre.
>
> Their condition there is such that no words can express the horror of it. That is the unanimous testimony of the rare traveller who have succeeded in visiting the camps where the unhappy victims are dying off, between Aleppo and Baghdad.
>
> I am not in a position to cite unimpeachable testimony as to the facts of these unheard-of atrocities.

A Turkish army-physician, Dr. H. Toroyan—an Armenian by birth, as appears by his name—was commissioned by the Young Turk government to visit the exiles' camps. The horrors of which he was a helpless witness in the course of his mission, and the hideous scenes at which he was present affected him so deeply that he determined to make his way out of Turkey, at the risk of his life, in order to reveal to the civilized world the barbarity and infamy of the guilty parties— that is, of the present rulers of Turkey and their accomplices.

He proceeded to show me the notes which he had taken day by day in the course of his tour of inspection down the Euphrates. It is a long series of awful pictures—stories of murders and tortures and revolting rapes.

Within these few lines, strange lies, errors, and absurdities are lined up, mingled with some truths. The rest of the article paints two pictures, very much the same as the scenes extracted in the Armenian version prepared by Yesayan—one of which is the small section regarding the rape and suicide of a young teacher at the Meskene station. But what is ever more interesting are the lies, errors, and absurdities. First and foremost, Barby could not have met Toroyan in Erzerum in June of 1915. This is a simple mistake. Let us suppose that he had met him in June of 1916, somewhere. Toynbee did not catch this mistake of "June 1915" when he had the article translated from French to English and placed it in his *Blue Book*. Beyond this mistake, what Barby says about Toroyan is a pure absurdity. First, if Toroyan was a medical doctor, it is ridiculous to think that the Young Turk government would assign the position of examiner to an Armenian doctor who was passing by the camps of exiled Armenians. Why has Barby appealed to this type of remedy?—clearly because he is forced to lie. He could not explain to his French audience that his Armenian eyewitness— from whom he would collect his "irrefutable" proof—was traveling with a German officer along the Euphrates. There is no such character of a German officer in his article. It is completely erased. If the intention was to appeal to the conscience of a French reader, then it was not an option to suggest that there was a sympathizing and sympathetic German at [Toroyan's] side—this was a time of war with Germany. Knowing that Toroyan had presented himself as a "doctor" in his compilation in *Arev*, it is also possible to believe that—upon that first lie—he is forced to heap on a second one. He had the foresight to know that it was better to keep quiet about the German officer he was traveling with, and, subsequently, to also not disclose to Henry Barby how he escaped.

How does all this connect with Zabel Yesayan? The connection is that the French journalist had no way to read Toroyan's journals and to be informed of their content. However, he speaks of them in such a way as if he had read them himself. ("Then, Dr. Toroyan showed me the notations he made as an inspector, day after day, along the length of the Euphrates.") In all honesty, he needed a translator. No doubt, that translator was Zabel Yesayan. And so, the suspicion is the following: it is highly likely that Barby never actually met Toroyan and only came to know him through Zabel Yesayan's translations. Even if he might have met him, the sections that he refers to are based on Yesayan's written translations. In its essence, this is more than plausible. And this is why in the same year of *Korz* monthly—in the January and February issues of 1916—there was an Eastern Armenian intellectual named Garen Mikaelian, who had published the book *An Armenia Cut to Pieces* (Բօշոտուած Հայաստան). This was a series of heart wrenching stories—I wouldn't dare call them "short stories"—the subjects of which were collected either from orphans in the orphanages or from survivors who spoke on their behalf and told similarly horrific stories of the father of these young Armenian boys and girls.

In 1917, Zabel Yesayan translated these stories into French. For whom? Certainly, for Henry Barby. And this is what she writes to Garen Mikaelian in September of 1917: "Mr. Barby asked that I seek your permission [on a certain matter]: that in the French publication it may seem as though he has worked directly with you and not with me."[17] Is it understandable what is happening here? In order to have an impact on the "general reader," Yesayan conveys Barby's wish in a manner that makes it appear that Barby had a real-life and direct interview with Mikaelian—this is so Barby's articles could appear as ones which "come from a direct source," and not a piece of writing extracted from a monthly journal that has been translated into French. One might ask: What does it matter, if, in the end, he did not mention that his work was based on an already existing and published work that was translated to French? What difference would it make, when he told the story of suffering children, whether the information was

---

[17] Zabel Yesayan, *Letters*, 143–4.

given to him by an eyewitness or from the direct source? What difference would it have made if he quietly skipped over the fact that he did not know the language of the victims and, in that case, needed a translator? What would be the difference if the entire chain of the report was denounced to forgetfulness, and he made it seem that he had gathered the information about the events and happenings directly from survivors—leaving the impression that the entire exchange had happened verbally. Really, what is the difference? Yet again, would the reader actually call attention to the subtle face of this deception? The subtle part is that the request is expressed, then transmitted by the hand of Zabel Yesayan. That is to say that Yesayan was involved in this deception by the French journalist. She accepted it, took part in it, encouraged it—with a deadly complicity. The French journalist and the Armenian author, hand in hand, believed that it was possible, even necessary, to distort the details of the exchange, to erase the dimension of the written word, in order to have a stronger impact on civilized society and to awaken the conscience of humanity. The voice of the interviewee had to reach the reader directly; a fake immediacy needed to be created—without the written, without the literary, without a go-between, without a translation. Taking part in this deception, Zabel Yesayan erases herself. She erases herself as a *woman*, as a *woman of letters*, as an *Armenian*, and as a *translator*.

Therefore, Barby's article was never going to make an appearance in the *Le Journal* newspaper without the help and participation of Zabel Yesayan as translator. It is clear that Yesayan chose the sections [that Barby included]—sections which Toroyan had most likely written down in his diaries—and had published as part of his pieces in *Arev*. Yesayan had edited these and had translated these [sections] for Barby. What could Barby have even done with Toroyan's diaries if it wasn't for Yesayan? The matter is not so much the dishonesty of a French journalist, but more so Zabel Yesayan's mindful participation. The suspicion grows stronger when we reflect on how Zabel Yesayan, explicitly, deriving from Toroyan's diaries, but erased their existence—and therefore the [first] written stage [of the work], Toroyan's initial attempts—and presented it as such that Toroyan had transmitted his story to her, orally. Barby's work erases the intercessions [of Toroyan's story], which immediately creates an illusion of immediacy for the French reader. Yesayan's work—her intervention with the diaries, on the written—is also erased to fashion an immediacy of orality.

I said earlier: "Zabel Yesayan . . . erases herself as a *woman*, as a *woman of letters*, as an *Armenian*, and as a *translator*." Why as a woman? That is what needs to be explained now. This was not the first time, of course, that Yesayan erased herself as a woman. In 1903, when she returned to Constantinople from Paris, she began to write for *Tzaghik* newspaper—these articles were imbued with a gentle and innocent feminism. In the same paper she published a short novel / novella, entitled *Vebu* [*The Novel*]. The story is about a young Armenian woman who returns to her home in Constantinople. There, she writes her first novel, and completely disgusted by its reception—or more accurately its lack of reception and exposure (*արձագանքի պակասէն*)—she leaves the city with the promise to never return again. Yes, we know: in her early period Yesayan's topics were very transparent in their autobiographical undertones. Let us suppose that, through this novel, Yesayan was trying to express the inner fears of a young writer and to overcome the emotional scars left from failure. In addition, the subject matter of the novel is also significant. Inspired by Goethe's *Wahlverwandschaften* (thought Yesayan most likely read the work in French), the story is about love. A woman's love dies. The woman later gets married, has a child—but the child, in the most shocking way, looks like the woman's former lover. The story can be interpreted as one where a woman becomes impregnated by a phantom or a ghost (*կինչ մը յոի ձգուիլը ուրուականի կամ կենդանի մեռելի մը կողմէ*)—by someone who survives their own death.

This is Zabel Yesayan's first novel written in Armenian. She wrote it during her years in Paris after she had written many pages (prose, poetry, and novels) in French. But *Vebu* [*The Novel*] entitled novel had another unique quality to it: it was printed without the name of an author. The result was, of course, that the reader would neither know who the author was nor to which sex they belonged. A man or a woman? Yesayan would conceal her sex. But in doing so, and in such an evident way, she was concealing the fact that she was a woman. Later on, one of her acquaintants, in the pages of the same *Tzaghig*, both revealed the identity of the author and explained its reasoning: that Yesayan had erased her name to conduct some sort of experiment and to be in the position to observe and record the impressions and effects of the novel and [to observe readers'] reactions. In this way, the reactions would be free from the coaxing expectations of the readers of her time regarding a woman writer. The uncertainty around the identity and sex of the author is the first, to my knowledge, of this type of notable expression [displayed] by Zabel Yesayan for a question that runs its course throughout her entire life (*Զաբէլ Եսայեանի մօտ ամբողջ կեանքի մը վրայ երկարող հարցադրութեան մը*): What could that be for a writer who is a woman? Must it have its own discerning qualities? Must it speak to what women of the time were facing? Is it acceptable, or even desirable, to say "I," or have a woman say "I"?

Or should it be molded into the fashion of a pure testimony—to endow the pen with the voice of a woman? Or is that through the writing that a woman should endow her pen with her real voice, with her womanly voice, and in this way become her own reporter who speaks in the first person? And, of course, if the one speaking is a woman, the pen does not need to be womanly. Or the reverse. Yes, the reverse. Whether the speaker is a woman or a man, how would one know if the hand who holds the pen is that of a woman? There is only one way. To sign [that writing] with the name of a woman, especially if the woman who is signing her name is doing nothing more than recording a testimony—to pronounce the voice which claims "I" by putting it on the page. And now, all of a sudden, what we find is that Zabel Yesayan's persistent and self-reflexive questioning around women's literature (or more preferably, around writing) is never disengaged from testimony, from the forms and manners of testimony, from the questions around the nature of testimony—that same testimony, which we now know does not separate the speaker from the recorder, creating an unbreakable bond, while at the same time always assuring a distinction between the two, even if both [the speaker and the one recording] are the same person.

From 1909 to 1911, and then from 1915 to 1922 or even further, Zabel Yesayan never stopped writing testimonies, or recording them and translating them. At the same time, she never stopped writing about women—and through this, she deepened her contemplations around the nature of the essence of "I" when it [that "I"] is a woman. And so, the author's [Yesayan's] exploration—an exploration of identity and gender runs parallel with a questioning about the essential-structural distinction between the female pen and the female voice. These experimentations, explorations, and interrogations would naturally hit a dead end in real life. One astonishing and almost unbelievable example of these inexplicable circumstances is the report that Zabel Yesayan authored in 1915 when she finally reached Bulgaria, after moving from one hiding place to another for three months in Constantinople. I am going to begin from here. The matter here is writing a testimony in first person. Do we have such an example?

We have a narration that appears in the form of a letter, which was not intended for publication. From April to August of 1915, Yesayan was living in secret among friends. Then, figuring she should not put her friends in danger, she lived in a hospital—from where she had to also escape when a Turkish soldier spotted her and recognized her. In August, disguised as a Turkish woman, she was able to obtain a passport. Here is what she writes, in this regard, from Filibe [current day Plovdiv] to her sister Geghoohi, who was living in Paris:

> It would be too lengthy for me to go into the details of what kind of horrors and frightful things we went through. My poor mother has been in mourning for three months because of my situation. It was only three months ago that I was living like a fugitive and I would come home sometimes, in secret. Only God knows what we have endured. Finally—through boldness, clever skills, and cold-heartedness—I was able to save myself with a miracle. Imagine my joy when I was finally able to cross the border. . . . In the end, I was walking on thorns trying to get out of that cursed place. May God save all of them. I was so emotional when I first set my eyes on Bulgaria. Praise Bulgaria![18]

Hrant Yesayan, who was five years old at the time, was able to join her mother later, and together they moved on to the Caucasus. Fifty years later, in a long and touching memoir, he wrote about those years—when he traveled from one side of the world to the other with his mother.[19]

Has Zabel Yesayan published the story of her escape anywhere? She has, yes, during those years: in *Hayastan* newspaper that was printed in Sofia. But what she published there is not what we would refer to as "testimony" today. It is based on facts, but it is a fictional report, written in first person and signed "Vicken"—as in the name of a man. This was not the first time, of course, that Zabel Yesayan had used a male pen name. However, the object in question here is not a work that is passing through the claws of Ottoman censorship, nor is it one where the use of a male pen name is intended to meet or go around the public expectations of its readership. It is the story of a wanderer in Constantinople, written in a completely realistic way, and as real-life events. This realistic and real narrative suddenly becomes something fictional, only following the change in gender. It is, of course, possible to assume that Zabel Yesayan was forced to hide her identity—and for the most part, to distort the details of her escape—in order to keep those living in Constantinople from harm. But she was also not required to write. This change in identity would have been attributed to discretion—if we did not know the great extent of her experiments related to the identity of male / female; if we did not also know about her questioning around writing-women and the complex position she took around testimony, to the point that they ran structurally parallel. Between extraction and translation, between the voice and the pen wavers [the two] which run parallel. (*Արտագրումին և թարգմանութեան միջև, ձայնին ու գրիչին միջև տատութեկուած զուցահեն մը:*).

---

[18] Zabel Yesayan, *Letter*, 119.
[19] Hrant Yesayan, "Zabel, my mother . . ." *Soviet Literature*, Yerevan, March 1978.

Let us also note that Yesayan's fictional report remained unfinished, because the newspaper *Hayastan* stopped being printed from September 26, 1915; this is when Bulgaria decided to take part in the war alongside Germany and Turkey. The signature "Vicken" appears for the first time in the August 15 issue of the newspaper, under an announcement of the death of Krikor Zohrab. The story of Yesayan's escape begins in the August 26 issue and continues for nine more issues.[20] Here is an excerpt from this issue. I draw attention to this to simply call to mind the strange consequences that appear when the identity of a gender is changed:

> When I got home, my wife's worries and her nervous anxiety put me in a different state. I wanted to give her assurance, but there was bad news being delivered [to us] from everywhere. Many had come by, interested in knowing more about me, and this had provoked her worry even more. My youngest was playing in the garden and [the child's] pure voice and joyous exclamations would pain my heart.... All of a sudden, I felt extreme vexation. What kind of fate is this? How many times does all this have to be destroyed...? As eternally illegitimate children of this country, why do we consider after all of us escaping, after hare-brained migrations [out of this place]—to return back to this cursed land, where every sacred endeavor turns even more suspicious to us all.... And we thought that with the establishment of the constitutional regime that we had finally reached our seaport.[21]

This is both an enticing and disturbing thing to witness: how Zabel Yesayan could take advantage of the most horrid moments to transform herself to appear as a man, in a written work that has a testimonial nature. Who is the one holding the pen here and who is the one telling the story? In the last issue of *Hayastan* newspaper, Yesayan describes how she has found a way to escape those after her. With the help of a doctor, to hide for a while in the hospitals of Constantinople: "he was to take me in as a patient in his establishment," she says. Given the circumstances, this was something I imagine was not hard to fake: "with days filled with sadness, anger, anxiety, along with my weak heart—[all this] had made me pretty sick already."[22] But back then, the male character, who spoke in first

---

[20] Hayastan newspaper started to be printed again in 2005, in Antilias, with the efforts of Jirair Tanielian. The material that helped to revive these efforts did not include number 54. The current publication offers a complete printing of the issues, thanks to the copy provided by the Armenians of the Vienna Mkhitarist order.
[21] Hayastan, Sofia, no. 50, September 2, 1915.
[22] Hayastan, September 26, 1915.

person, was naturally unable to explain from where he was acquainted with the Turkish soldier who had recognized him, informing him of the threat of being exposed. Here, the first person really becomes something fictitious—what was being described was not written with any intention of being as such. Years later, during Soviet times, Yesayan would play other games around identity and gender / sex—even more mind-blowing than this one. For example, in her last extensive novel *The Gardens of Silihdar*, in Parba Khachig, she was going to borrow the scenes and ambience, in order to recreate the childhood of the young character. In this case, the change between genders does not have a direct correlation with the testimonial. But it is important to remember that the published version of *Parba Khachig*—despite its uncharacteristic length—is a censured novel. The events are interrupted in the year 1914, and then the story begins again in 1918, as if nothing happened between those years. As if the censorship between 1896 to 1908 was not enough, as if Young Turks' policy of extermination was not enough, a silence and propaganda of Kemalist Turkey that attempted to erase the past, but also Armenians, through their own will, had to become subject to another type of censorship—the censorship imposed by the Soviet regime—where they once again had to erase their past from their production of literature and the testimony. Those who explore the limits of literature and testimony still have a lot of work to do. And this is all the more the reason that Zabel Yesayan erased herself, as a woman, when writing testimony.

But as always, the one who is erased always resurfaces, in different ways. She resurfaced when she withstood the obligation of testimony in *The Agony of a People*; [she did this] by choosing not to translate it to French, by signing with her (a woman's) name, and by freeing it from its original form, as a document. And she was going to resurface again, yet in another way, which was just as impactful and just as convictive. In the same letter addressed to Garen Mikaelian—where she worked toward erasing her role as a translator, as she relayed the request of Henry Barby and succumbed to immediacy and imperative—she says also the following:

> As soon my work becomes lighter, I will begin writing a novel about the life of Armenians in Constantinople, with the title of *My Soul in Exile*. I am fed up with the subject of this novel, and as soon as I am alone—which is an uncommon occurrence—I will withdraw to this part of my soul, which is where my novel's world exists it seems. There, destruction, exiled, Bolshevik and other such things do not exist; rather, there is only sun, roses, perpetual songs of love, beauty

and grace. If I could even express a small part of this hidden world, I will feel gratified, most gratified.[23]

This "novel" was actually written in these years and was published in 1922 under the title of *My Soul in Exile*. This is where Zabel Yesayan reinvents the "women's writing" to its fullest, completely reviving the inspiration of the novella she wrote in previous years. It is a woman who speaks in the first person, in the competition recorded in the novellas / novels. Beyond the unlawful atmosphere of rivalry, hatred, and separation described in the novellas *Սոյորում* and *The Passing Times*, she moves past the character of a painter that put herself in competition with her husband. 1917 was the year that she had completely committed herself to the organization of those heart-wrenching testimonies and their translation into French, when, along with the sympathy of humanity, her powerless resistance դիմադրմունքիւնը could have devoured her essence completely, as she fully worked toward erasing herself as a woman and as a writer—and so it is that same year that Zabel Yesayan would come to assign to her most beautiful and sparkling characters a woman, in the first person. Against the obligations of testimony, against the expectation to shake the conscience of civilized society, she had to protect the rights of her "minority" language, along with her place as author and the legitimacy of her written work. But there was a fourth layer, a fourth scope, that had to be protected just as much as the others: and that is the uniqueness of being a woman. She had to defend her distinction as woman, as much as she had to defend her language, the author, and the literature. We would have never known [any of this] if there never lived this extraordinary woman, with the name of Zabel Yesayan, in her 1917 "agony" of a people and with her soul in "exile." She might have erased her name through testimony (but she also resisted, and through her resistance she freed the testimonial); she worked toward her own erasure, as a woman, as an author, and as the inhabitant of an unfamiliar language that appealed to the human conscience. She drew attention to her erasure. She assumed that there was no connection between that and the expanding desire across the border to strangle the soul of her people. She had to return by coming back, to the rosebushes of Skuidar (Üsküdar), to Istanbul, to the twilight of the Bosphorus, to art, and to motions of love. This is where she would escape from being erased. This is where she would reestablish the distinction. The matter was not simply to secure a beautiful island in the sea of terror *սարսափներու ովկեանին մէջ*. It wasn't the terror that forced her

---

[23] *Letters*, 144.

to take a step back, toward the heady rosebushes, toward the creative. It was testimony. The testimonial as an erasure of difference returned her to the craft, as an inscription of difference. One by one, and continuing, much later, she has had the same type of confidence, the same type of splendor, but independent of testimony. When she wrote the character of Melia Nuri Hanem, she gave voice to a Turkish woman [by putting her] in first person. And she signed it: Zabel Yesayan.

Index

Adana, Ottoman province   xviii, xxv, 15, 19, 25
Adana Massacres   xxv, 15, 25
Adyghe; *see* Circassians
Agony of a People, The   xix, xxviii–xxix, 137–57
Aintab   14–16, 15 n.7
   agriculture   16
   Armenians in   15
   deportation of people   16–17
   economy   16
   handcrafts   16
   Kurdish in   15
   Turkish in   15
   viticulture   16
Aintoura Orphanage   xxvi n.10
Ajemian, Levon Bey   75
Akçura, Yusuf (1876–1935)   xxvi n.13
Aktokmakyan, Maral   4 n.4
Aleppo   xxix, 6, 44–5, 48–9, 65–9, 65 n.3
   Armenian deportees from western *vilayets* in   79
   Armenian population   75–81
   Armenians from Sueda in   79
   banks   76
   Christians in   75
   government   77–8
   market   75–6
   Muslim Arabs in   75
   population of   75
   refugees from Cilicia in   76–7
   Rod al-Faraj inn   80
   schools/colleges   76
   Tashnags   79, 79 n.4
   women and children deportees in   77
Allah khadru ichun (For the love of God)   116
alla turca time   103 n.1
Amasya   47
Among the Ruins (Yesayan)   xviii–xxi
Anchrti village, Arapgir   65, 65 n.1
Anē   117, 117 n.1

Arab tribe of Anez   46–7, 46 n.9
Arapgir   65
Arap Punar   9, 52, 61, 63, 80
Armenian cemetery   103–7
Armenian Church of Yerortutiun (Holy Trinity) in Pera   xxiv
Armenian communities   xxiii–xxiv
Armenian *fedayi*/resistance movement   xxiv
Armenian *gendarme*   11–12
Armenian General Benevolent Union (AGBU)   77, 77 n.2
Armenian genocide   xxiii–xxix
Armenian girls   86–7, 89–90
   in Birecik   89–90
   as bravery   89–90
   corpses of   87
   as gift   14, 54
   Turkish/Kurdish propaganda against   89–90
   wedding   89–90
Armenian market   4–5
Armenian mother   29–34
Armenians   38–9
   in Aintab   15
   in Aleppo   75–81
   in Anē   117
   in Baghdad   127–8
   bride's escape   65–6
   in Deir ez-Zor   109–12
   deportation   21–7, 41–9
   deportees from Drabizon   68
   deportees from western *vilayets*   79
   of Dikranagerd   3–8, 41–9
   in Dört-yol   13, 13 n.4
   dying in Mesopotamia   1–2
   Edessa (Urfa)   83–8
   emigrants   22
   from Erzrum   66–9
   in Hadise   119–20
   in Hajn   13, 13 n.3
   in Hīt   121–2

in Jarābulus 9–12, 22–4
for *kurban* (sacrifice) 39
of Marash 19
massacres 41
in Meskene 97–101
passing through Birecik 71–4
in Persia 129–35
in Ramadi 121, 123
in Raqqa 103–7
resistance xxv, 83–8
from Samsat 38
from Sueda 79
in Suruji ova (Plain of Suruj) 51–2
thrown into river 36–9
women xxv, 21–5, 41
in Zeytun 13–14, 13 n.2, 123
Armenian tailors 5
Armenian village 21–7
   deportation and 21–7
   deportees 21–7
   exports of pistachios 21
   income 21
   Kurdish assault in 21
   nighttime assaults 25–7
   search and plunder in 21–2
   trees 21
   women/children 21–5
Arnavuts 43, 43 n.4
Assyrians 3, 42
atrocities xxv
   Balkan xxvi
authorship 137–57

Bafra 47
Baghdad 42, 127–8
Balkans xxvi
Balkan Wars (1912–13) xxvi, 4
Bapron 57
Ba'qūbah 129, 129 n.2, 130
bedel 68, 68 n.7
Benevolent Society 77
berader (brother) 73, 73 n.7
Bey, Khaled 45
Bey, Memduh 5, 42
Bey, Mustafa 25, 27
Birecik 7 n.10, 14, 17, 29, 38–9
   Armenians conversion to Islam 90–1
   Armenians passing through 71–4
   fire 7
   residents 89

Bitlis 42
Boyadjian, Tamar Marie 4 n.4
bride's escape 65–6
Bunbuj 86

caravan of deportees 22–3
Catholicos of Cilicia 13
çetes [armed bands] 43, 43 n.3
Chavush, Nazaret 13–14, 13 n.5
Chechen *reisi* 80, 80 n.7
Chechens 10–11, 41–3, 147
Chemeshgadzak 63–4
Cherkess; *see* Circassians
Chermug 46, 46 n.7
Chnkush 46, 46 n.6
Chrajian, Stepan 7, 7 n.9
Christians
   Muslim animosity against xxvi
   perpetrator xxvi
Christian Syrians 49
Christian xenophobia xxviii
Cilicia 13–19
   Catholicos of 13
   deportations in 13–19
   massacres (1909) xviii–xix, xxi
Circassians 10–11, 25–6, 25 n.5, 43, 86
Committee of Union and Progress (CUP) 4 n.4
conversions 90–1
corpses 36–8
counterrevolutionary movement xxv

Damascus 85
davul 90, 90 n.2
Dayi, Ali 24, 24 n.4, 35
death xix–xx
   as political animal xxi
   throes xxii
Deir ez-Zor 107, 109 n.1
   Armenians in 109–12
   market 113–16
deportation (*tehcir*) xxvii
   of Armenians 21–7, 41–9
      to Arap Pınar 47–9
      to Dikranagerd 41–2
      to Edessa (Urfa) 47
      on foot toward Aleppo 65–9
      to Jarābulus (Syria) 9–12, 22–4, 57–64
      to Mardin 42–3

to Resulayn 43–5
to Tell Abyad 45–7, 45 n.5
by train 57–64
in Cilicia 13–19
of Yerznga 57–63
Deutsche Orientbank 76
Dikranagerd 3–8, 80
  Armenian market in 4–5
  Armenians 3–8, 41–9
  Armenian villages in 3, 5–6
  bankers 41
  Birecik fire 7
  Christians, economic boycott of 4
  as commercial center of north-eastern provinces 3
  economy 4
  inhabitants 3–4
  Ittihadists and 4–5
  Kurds in 3–8
  military in 5
  Muslim inhabitants 3–4
  Turks in 3–8
distribution of bread 35–6
divide-and-rule policy xxiv
Diyarbakir xxix
Dörtyol, Armenians in xxv, 13–15, 13 n.4
Drabizon, Armenian deportees from 68
dying breath xx, xxii
dying song xxii
Dzag kar 42, 42 n.2

earmels 124, 124 n.2
Edessa (Urfa) 9, 14, 41, 41 n.1, 46–7, 71, 80–1, 83–8, 91, 93, 95
  Armenians 83–8
  Armenian women 83–4
  assault on Armenian quarter 86–8
  deportation of 83–8
  Kurds from 86–8
  resistance 83–8, 95
  Turks from 86–8
  violent massacre (1895) 87–8
Effendi, Hasan 25, 27, 71
Effendi, Koynopulos 30, 31
elegy (*meni*) 23, 23 n.2
embroidery society 88
Erznga 63, 67
Erzrum, Armenians from 66–9
Euphrates 21–2, 25, 35–6

Fallujah 122, 122 n.3
fezzes 23, 23 n.3
First World War xxiii

gâvur 72 n.3
gendarmes 5–6, 10–11, 17–18, 21–6, 33–4, 41, 43–4, 46–8, 51–2, 62–3, 67–9, 73, 89, 94, 99–101, 103–5, 107, 111, 119, 124, 131, 133–4
Gerason 57
German hospital, Jarābulus 93–5
Gesaria 48, 48 n.11
Ghurban ellam! 113, 113 n.1
ghurush 16, 16 n.10, 58
Gökalp, Mehmed Ziyâ (1876–1924) xxvi n.13
Greek Catholics 49
Greek-Turkish population xxvii–xxviii

Hadise 119–20, 119 n.1
Hadjin xxv, 13 n.3
Hajin 85
Hajn, Armenians in 13, 13 n.3, 15
ḥalāl 21, 21 n.1
Halil *bey* 43, 80
Hama 18–19
Hamid II, Abdul (r. 1876–1909) xxiv–xxv
Hamidiye Massacres (1894–6) xxiv
Hamidiye regiments 48 n.10
hanem 32, 32 n.5
Hanike 130
Harunabad 132, 132 n.9
Hauran 14
Hauran desert 14
Hay Heghapokhagan Tashnagtsutyun (Armenian Revolutionary Federation) 79, 79 n.4
Hīt 121–2, 121 n.1
Hnchakian 7
hokevark xix–xx, xxii
Holy Saviour 11
Homs 18–19
human xviii
  condition xviii, xxi
  life xviii, xx
  for Armenians xviii
  quality of xviii–xix

infidel 72 n.3
Islamic Shop (*Maghazayi islamie*) 4
Islamized Armenians 90–1
Istanbul xviii, 91, 95
Ittihadists 4

Jarābulus (Syria) xxix, 9–12, 22, 29
  Armenians in 9–12, 22–4, 57–64
  bazaar 52–4
  German hospital at 93–5
  kaymakam 11–12, 11 n.4, 24
  mobilization and military requisitions in 10
  non-Muslim schools in 10
  Turks in 9–12

kāfir 72 n.3
Kangavar 134, 134 n.10
Karadagh forest 11, 38, 38 n.3
Kavafian 68–9
kaymakam 11–12, 11 n.4, 18, 24, 27, 30, 35, 67, 97
  of Adıyaman 12
kaymakam bey 30–4
Kemakh 68
Kemakhi Boghaz 62, 62 n.3
Kerend 132, 132 n.8
Kermanshah 129–35
khan 46, 46 n.8, 97
Kharpert 16, 43, 46, 127
Khaser Shirin 131
khāyins 18, 18 n.12
kiwlah 53, 53 n.3
Konya 106
*külah*s 53
kurban (sacrifice) 39, 39 n.5
Kurban olayım 113, 113 n.1
Kurds/Kurdish xxiii, 65, 67, 89
  in Aintab 15
  from Edessa (Urfa) 86–8
  "Hamidiye" forces xxiv
  plunder to women of Armenia 41, 71
  wedding among 89–90

Lausanne Treaty (1923) xxviii
League of Nations supervision xxviii
life as labor xviii
local begs 68, 68 n.6
lolig 52, 52 n.2

Mahmud *Onbashi* 51–2, 51 n.1
Malatia 16, 16 n.9, 68
Marash 14, 100
  Armenians of 19
  Armenian villagers 109–12
  reservists from 14
  Süleymanlı in 13 n.2
  Turkish soldier from 91
Mardin 41–3
  Armenians deportation (*tehcir*) to 42–3
  women and girls 42
Mardiros Atarian's silk factory 6
Matossian, Bedross Der xxv
Mdzpin (Nusaybin) 10, 10 n.3, 44, 45
mejid 33, 33 n.6
*meni*s 33, 33 n.7
Mersin 19
Meskene 97–101
Mesopotamia 1–2, 27, 78, 87
Miller, Owen Robert xxiv
Mosul 127
Mother Armenia in chains 54, 54 n.4
mudir 110, 110 n.2
muhajir (refugee) 72
mülazım (lieutenant) 131, 131 n.4
Murad 71–4, 71 n.1
Murat's Journey (*from Sivas to Batum*) xix
Musa Bey xxiii–xxiv
Muslims 3–4, 51–2
  refugees (*muhacirler*) xxvi
  religious identity xxvi, xxvi n.12
  supremacy xxvi

Nahr-el-Baquba river 130
Nichanian, Marc xix, xxi, 137, 137 n.2
Nizib khan 54–6, 54 n.5, 85
non-Muslim Christian communities xxviii
Nor Sepastia xix

Oehlmann, Otto 93–4, 114, 128, 131–3, 139, 141–2
Oghli, Hoja 73
oka 98, 98 n.2
olmaz 30, 30 n.2
"Orphanages of Cilicia, The" xix

Ottoman Armenian community xxiii–xxiv
Ottoman Bank 88
Ottoman biopolitical state xxvii
Ottoman constitution 15–16, 75, 88
Ottoman Empire xx–xxi
Ottoman Gendarmerie 5, 5 n.6
Ottoman pound 6 n.7
Ottoman state violence xxiii

pain xix
paras 58, 58 n.2
Pasha, Cemal xxvi, xxvi n.10
Pasha, Enver xxvi
Pasha, Fakhri 14, 19, 85
Pasha, Jemal 13, 19, 27, 78–80, 85
Pasha, Talaat xxvi–xxvii, 90 n.4
Paypert 67, 67 n.5
Persia 129–35
plunder 5, 7, 11, 21–2, 25–7, 41–2, 46, 51–3, 76, 84, 86–7, 110
political violence xxv
priests 15
properties 90
Puzantion daily 90, 90 n.3

Qasr-e Shirin 131, 131 n.5

Ramadi 121–2, 121 n.1
Raqqa 97, 97 n.1, 99, 103–7
    Armenians in 103–7
    corpses in 104–5
red egg 65, 65 n.2
ressentiment xxviii, xxviii n.19
Resulayn 10–11, 10 n.2, 41, 43–5, 64, 79
Rumelian Turkish refugees 14
Rumkale 35, 35 n.1
Russian assault 135
Russian Cossacks 95

Sahag Catholicos 13
Sajur 16, 16 n.11
Samsak 57
Samsat 68–9
Samsun 47
Sarpul 131, 131 n.6
self-defense campaigns xxv

Sepasdia 16, 57, 57 n.1, 127
Serengulian, Vartkes 80, 80 n.6
sevab (acceptable to God) 71, 71 n.2, 89
Sevk ve İskân Kanunu (Relocation and Resettlement Law) xxvii
Shahraban 130, 130 n.3
shalwars 106, 106 n.2
Sheikh al-Islam 91
sheikhs 89
Shmavonian, Samuel 77, 77 n.2
Siirt 43
Sis 19, 19 n.13
Sivas 47
Siverek 9, 9 n.1, 41, 46
siwlfat te kinin 116, 116 n.2
Social Democratic *Hnchak* [Bell] Party 7 n.9
sorrow xix
Subḥān-Allāh 77 n.1
Sueda, Armenians from 79
Suedia 79, 79 n.3
suffering xix
Supurgiji (Surp Prgich) 38, 38 n.4
Suq Haradize 132, 132 n.7
Suruji ova (Plain of Suruj) 51–2
    as Armenian cemetery 52
    Armenians in 51–2
    Kurds in 51–2
    Muslims in 51–2
    Turks in 51–2
Syrian Desert xxvii

Tabriz 131
Talat *bey* 90, 90 n.4
tasbīḥ 77 n.1
Tashnags 79, 79 n.4
teachers 15, 99
Tehran xxix
Tell Abyad 45–7, 45 n.5
Teotig, Arshaguhi (1875–1922) xxv
testimony 137–57
torment xix
Toroyan, Hayg xix–xx, 1
    and Armenian genocide xxiii–xxix
    testimony xxiii–xxix
Toroyan, Hayk xx–xxi
Trabzon 47
Turkishness xxvi, xxvi n.12, xxviii

Turks/Turkish   1–2, 38–9, 68, 71, 83, 89
    in Aintab   15
    in Edessa   81
    from Edessa (Urfa)   86–8
    ethnonationalism   xxvi, xxvi n.13
    serviceman   14
    soldiers   6, 14, 14 n.6, 36, 42–4, 51,
        58, 61, 87, 141
    suspicious attitude toward local
        Armenians   93–5

Üngör, Uğur Ümit   xxviii

vartabeds   15, 15 n.8

water   57–8
wild tribes (*aşair-i mutavahhişe*)   xxvii
women of Armenia   xxv, 21–5, 41
    assaulted by Chechens   41
    as booty   51
    deportation (*tehcir*) to Jarābulus
        (Syria)   57–64
    furious and obstinate   83–4
    hanging from her feet   42
    Kurds plunder to   41, 72

yavrum   26, 26 n.6
yazma   32, 32 n.4
Yedikardashian brothers   84

Yerznga   16, 57–64
Yesayan, Zabel (1879–1943)   xviii–xxii,
    xxv, xxviii–xxx, xxviii n.21, 1,
    137–57
    Agony of a People, The   xix
    Among the Ruins   xviii–xxi
    authorship   137–57
    brilliance   xxi–xxii
    *Murat's Journey (from Sivas to
        Batum)*   xix
    Nor Sepastia   xix
    preface   xxi
    testimonies   xix, 137–57
    Toroyan's testimony   xix
    transcription of survivor
        testimony   xxix
    as writer   xx
yesir   72, 72 n.5

zaptı; *see* Ottoman Gendarmerie
Zeytun   85
    Armenians in   13–14, 13 n.2, 121–2
    four city councilmen imprisoned
        13–14
Zifteg   64
Zohrab, Krikor   80, 80 n.6
zulm   77 n.1
zulüm   77 n.1
zurna   90, 90 n.2

www.ingramcontent.com/pod-product-compliance
Lightning Source LLC
Chambersburg PA
CBHW050802160426
43192CB00010B/1611